The
Santa Claus
Book

The Santa Claus Book

Alden Perkes

Illustrations by the Author

Lyle Stuart Inc.
Secaucus, New Jersey

Library of Congress Cataloging in Publication Data
Perkes, Alden.
  The Santa Claus book.
  Summary: Presents information about Santa
Claus and his associates, including how he gets
all those toys into the bag; where Mrs. Claus
comes from; and why Santa lives so long.
  1. Santa Claus. 2. Christmas [1. Santa
Claus. 2. Christmas] I. Title.
GT4992-P47 1982   818'.5407   82-10241
ISBN 0-8184-0327-6

First edition
All rights reserved.
No part of this book may be reproduced in any form
whatsoever except by a newspaper or magazine reviewer
who wishes to quote brief passages in connection
with a review.

Queries regarding rights and permissions should
be addressed to: Lyle Stuart Inc., 120 Enterprise
Ave., Secaucus, N.J. 07094.

Published by Lyle Stuart Inc. Published simultaneously
in Canada by Musson Book Company, a division of
General Publishing Co. Limited, Don Mills, Ontario.

Printed and bound by Tien Wah Press(Pte.) Ltd.,
Singapore.

Copyright © by Information Design

Illustrations copyright © 1982 by Information Design

"It's Christmas All the Year," p. 25, copyright © 1982 by Information
Design and Michael F. Moody.

This book was created at Information Design,
Inc. It was produced through the joint efforts of:

Larry Belliston—Developer/Planner
Kurt Hanks—Director
Jay A. Parry—Editor/Writer
Steve Songer—Illustrator
Marge Neuharth—Production Artist
Michael F. Moody—Musical Composer
Pat Ferguson—Musical Composer
Vicki Hughes—Cookie Consultant
Corinne Reed—Cookie Poem
Santa Claus—Technical Consultant
Zeeker—Ass't. Technical Consultant

**"This is the most correct book on Santa I've
ever seen. It's the only one I authorize. Alden
has done a wonderful job, and I commend this
book to all readers everywhere. Ho! Ho! Ho!"**

Santa

Acknowledgments

My sincerest thanks are expressed to all the people who helped make this book possible:

To **Santa Claus,** who so thoughtfully shared with me his time and hospitality at the North Pole during my many, many visits there.

To **Mrs. Santa,** a real Princess, who bakes the best muffins north of the South Pole, for the many fine meals, the clean sheets, and the heart-to-heart talks.

To **the elves,** especially Zeeker, Raful, Amt, and Gald, who shared with me their expertise on such varied matters as loading a sleigh, talking to a reindeer, and the genealogical background of the elvish species.

To **the reindeer,** for being patient while we talked through elvish interpreters; and for the special air show they put on for me.

To **the Ice Nymphs,** for giving me back my pants after they'd stolen them.

To **all the special children** who helped me in the research and production of this work: Aaron, Amy, Brock, Casey, David, Dion, Jake, Jenny, JoAnna, Jonathan, Joshua, Katie, Melanie, Nathaniel, Sam, Sarah, Sunny, Trisha, and Troy.

And especially to **all the children of the world,** who know Santa Claus is the greatest guy around.

Contents

Gus is babysitting one of the fawns while the reindeer are away making the Christmas rounds with Santa.

The
Santa Claus
Book

Where Santa Came From

Once upon a time, when the world was much younger, a very special child was born. He came to be known as Santa Claus, and he's loved and revered the world over.

But the story begins even before then. In a quiet little village in a small country lived a handsome young carpenter named Sandy Claus. His wife was named Tasha, and she was the most beautiful lady in the whole land. Sandy and Tasha were very happy together. They never quarreled; they were respected by their fellow villagers; they always had plenty of food to eat.

But there was one sadness in their lives, and it made their hearts ache. They wanted desperately to have a little child. But they'd never been able to.

Years passed, then passed again. Sandy was elected mayor of the village. Tasha became the best friend of all the children in the town. But still they had no child of their own.

Sandy's beard turned gray. Tasha began to have wisps of white in her hair. And they knew that they had become too old to have children now. Their dream would forever go unfulfilled.

One night before they went to bed, Sandy looked up at the sky. Black clouds moved ponderously across the stars. "It's going to be a bad one," he said solemnly. And he latched the shutters firmly over the windows. As the night wore on, the sky turned dark and wild. The wind moaned through the trees; leaves skittered down the dusty road.

"This is a night of nights!" Sandy whispered to Tasha. "It's enough to make strong men weep!"

The rain pelted down against their thatched roof, drowning out his words. But Tasha shared his fears, and clung close to him underneath their thick quilts.

The storm whipped about them hour after hour, as they tossed and turned through the endless night.

Then, suddenly, the rain stopped. The wind turned away. All was quiet. Sandy drew a deep breath. Tasha uttered a silent prayer of thankfulness.

But the wail began again. Only this time it was different. It didn't rustle the thatches on the roof; it didn't wheeze around the corners of the house. It was high and shrill—and very lonely.

During the worst part of the storm, a beautiful young woman left the baby Santa on the doorstep—and then fled back into the darkness.

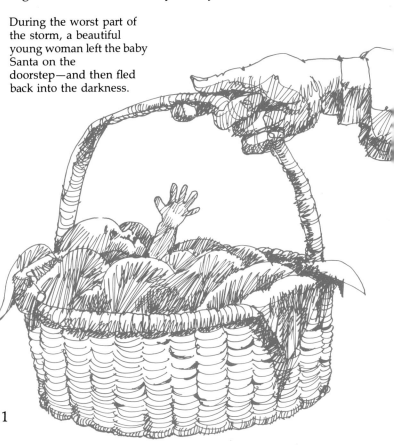

1

Tasha sat up in bed, urgent. "It's a baby!" she said. And she jumped out of the bed and ran ot the door of their hut. There, on their doorstep, was a little reddened baby wrapped in heavy blankets, soaked to the skin—and crying lustily. She picked him up tenderly, held him to her breast, and carried him to Sandy. "A baby," she said softly.

They pulled the wet blankets off. Attached to the baby's diaper was a note: "I love this baby more than my life. But disaster threatens! I know you will care for him as if he were your own. **Love him for me!**" The note was not signed.

Tasha held the baby's cheek against hers. "Something horrible has happened to your mother on this horrible night," she said. "But we will love and care for you, for *her*. Forever!"

In the morning, Tasha and Sandy had the first and last argument of their marriage. "We'll name the baby after me," Sandy announced at the breakfast table. "We'll call him Sandy."

Tash looked up sharply. "No," she said. "I've waited so long. We must call him Tash, after me."

"It will be Sandy." Sandy said again, his voice rising louder.

"No! Tash!" Tasha answered, her voice even louder.

They ate the rest of their meal in silence, avoiding glances, refusing to speak. Then the baby began to cry, and Tasha went to care for him. Sandy slammed the door when he left the hut to go to work.

All day long Tasha thought of the problem. "We both love this baby—but we love each other too. I was wrong. We should name him Sandy."

And all day long Sandy thought of the problem, as he sawed and hammered his wood. "I love Tasha more than myself," he thought. "I've been so wrong. We'll name him Tash."

When he went home that night, Tasha met him at the door. "We'll name him San—" she started to say but Sandy interrupted:

"Tash," he said.

Then they looked at each other and laughted. "Santash?" Sandy said. "What kind of a name is that?"

The adults thought Santa had too much elf blood in him, and they tried to chase him out of town.

"No kind of name for our son," Tasha said. "Why don't we name him Santa, after both of us?"

Santa was a good boy, helpful to his mother and obedient to his father. He made friends quickly as he grew, and soon he was the favorite among his fellows.

But the adults in the village were worried. "His ears are a little pointed," said one. "I'll bet he has some elf blood in him."

"I don't trust him," said another. "Never trust half-elf, that's what I always say."

"His cheeks are too rosy," gossiped a third. "Just like an elf's!"

When Santa walked into the village, the people called him names, and were rude to him. "Don't come near me, Elf-boy. I don't want your evil magic around me!"

"Get away from here, Imp!"

"Don't you dare look at me with your elvish evil-eye, you point-eared twit!"

More than once, Santa ran home crying to his mother. "I'm sorry," Tasha said. "I'm sorry." And she stroked his golden hair.

When he grew older, Tasha explained: "People are foolish," she said. "They fear elves because elves are different. But just by looking in your face I can tell they are a wonderful people."

While the adults were being mean, the children were becoming Santa's friends, more and more. They didn't care that his ears pointed a little; and they didn't care that his cheeks were rosy. All they knew was that he was a loving friend, and they loved him back.

Children have always loved Santa—even when he was a child himself.

3

When Santa became a man, he moved away from the village to another land, far away. He became a famous carpenter, with kings and princes coming to him for carpentry work.

But everywhere he went he saw meanness. People beating their children. Drinking or gambling away their money while their children went hungry. Buying a fine new horse or carriage while their children wore rags.

Of course, most parents were wonderful with their children. But when Santa saw the mean ones, he wept. And he remembered how his friends had loved him as a boy, when all the adults were horrible.

"I must help these poor children," he said to himself. And he began to save his money.

On the next gift-day, Santa took special gifts to all the poor children and left them in secret during the night. The next day the whole town was alive with talk of the miracle that had happened: some mysterious being had left gifts for many, many children in the night. Santa smiled to himself. And he felt happier than he ever had before.

The next year, Santa gave out even more gifts and the following year he gave still more. And he noticed that the people in the town began to change. No one knew who was giving the gifts—so everyone was kind to everyone else. "My wicked neighbor might be the generous one, in secret," each of the townspeople thought. "I'd better treat him much better." They were nicer to their children, too. "If someone thinks they're that special," they thought, "I should be kinder to them."

Before long, Santa was giving gifts to every child in the town. "I want every one of them to feel loved, by someone," he wrote in a letter to Sandy and Tasha. "I want every one of them to have as much love as you gave me."

As Santa gave more and more, he wanted to share with even more children. He wanted to give to every child in the land, and in the neighboring land, and in all the lands beyond that. And, over the years, he's been able to do just that.

Now the little boy who was left on the doorstep in the storm, the little boy who was half-elf, ridiculed by the people in his town—now that little boy is a man. Now he's Santa Claus, the most famous, most loved man in the whole world!

A Chat with Santa Claus

My moment had finally arrived—my "official," completely on-the-record interview with the world's most famous man, Santa Claus. He was dressed in a red suit, his portly frame lounging comfortably in his chair. His full white beard was groomed to perfection. I was a little nervous, but the twinkle in his eye set me at ease. I took a deep breath and began:

Alden: Santa, why do you think you've grown to be the most famous man in the entire world? After all, there are plenty of people who are doing good deeds. . . .

Santa: I think it's my red suit. Red is most people's favorite color.

Alden: Every year at Christmastime, merchandisers all over the world use your name and your image to sell their goods. Do you feel you're being exploited?

Santa: Not too much. But last year I had a talk with the Easter Bunny, and, boy, is he ever ticked off!

Alden: What do you do for money, Santa?

Santa: Well, I don't need much. We get most of our food from our summer garden. And most of the materials for toys are donated by good people all over the world.

Alden: When you do get money, where do you put it?

Santa: I put it in a snowbank once, but I lost it when I forgot which one. Or maybe the Ice Nymphs got it.

Alden: How do you get along with the elves?

Santa: Just great! Until I give them a job they don't like. Shoveling snow, for instance.

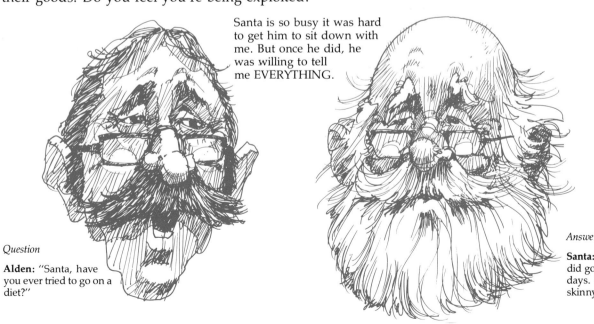

Santa is so busy it was hard to get him to sit down with me. But once he did, he was willing to tell me EVERYTHING.

Question

Alden: "Santa, have you ever tried to go on a diet?"

Answer

Santa: "Well, back in 1947 I did go off cookies for three days. But who wants a skinny Santa?"

5

Alden: If shoveling snow is their least favorite job, what's their most favorite?

Santa: Mowing the lawn.

Alden: I've always wondered—why are there no female elves?

Santa: Go smell the elves' breath some day and you'll have your answer! No, I'm just kidding. Female elves' breath is just as bad! Actually, there are female elves, and they live right here at the North Pole. I've overheard them talking a time or two. But I've never seen one. They're real sly about that.

Alden: When you go around the world, delivering all those presents, how do you get down the chimneys?

Santa: I make myself small.

Alden: And the presents, too?

Santa: Of course. A tiny person can't carry huge presents.

Alden: Is your miniscule size the reason why children can't see you when you visit?

Santa: You mean children can't see me? That's a shame!

Alden: Is your house about the same as other houses of the world?

Santa: Basically. Except I have a happiness room and a laughing room.

Alden: Does your laughing room really laugh?

Santa: No, *I* do. When I go in it. Just walking in puts me in stitches.

Alden: Are you really fat, or is that just the fit of your clothes?

Santa: I'm not fat. I come from a fat race, and among my people I'm skinny!

Alden: Who are your people?

Santa: I was orphaned as a baby, you know. But I suspect my genealogy traces back to the Wyrsters of the valleys of Yinlyn. They're quite famous in anthropological circles.

Alden: You've been credited with thousands of invaluable inventions, such as the chair and dog fur. What's the invention you're most proud of?

Santa: I'm proudest of the *clause.* It did wonders in enabling people to create intelligible sentences in speaking and writing. And it works in nearly all languages. I was so pleased with that one that I named it after myself. You don't sit on a clause, but you do speak with one!

Santa likes to use a lot of body language when he talks. It gives the conversation a lot of color.

How Old Is Santa?

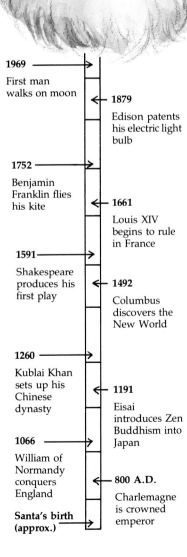

It's difficult to pin down Santa's birthdate for certain—but his memory extends back as far as the 700s! This timeline shows the incredible extension of Santa's life:

Present. Santa is known throughout the world as a man of great generosity and magnanimity.

Even at his present great age, Santa is expected to live for many more hundreds and thousands of years.

In Middle Age. Santa saves Limlim, the elf. Soon thereafter he obtained his first reindeer.

As a Young Man. Santa marries Princess Anwyn, saving her from a life as a barmaid.

Santa only made one bad mistake in his life (and I mean a really, really bad one), and it was—well, I promised not to say.

As a Boy. Santa begins his practice of giving gifts, sharing what little he has with others.

Santa was personally acquainted with such historical personages as Columbus and Edison, and he even helped them with their discoveries and inventions.

As a Baby. Santa is reared by loving foster parents.

1969
First man walks on moon

1879
Edison patents his electric light bulb

1752
Benjamin Franklin flies his kite

1661
Louis XIV begins to rule in France

1591
Shakespeare produces his first play

1492
Columbus discovers the New World

1260
Kublai Khan sets up his Chinese dynasty

1191
Eisai introduces Zen Buddhism into Japan

1066
William of Normandy conquers England

800 A.D.
Charlemagne is crowned emperor

Santa's birth (approx.)

Santa's Best-Kept Secret

Santa doesn't really want it that way, but Mrs. Santa is his best-kept secret. She's the one who makes things happen right up at the North Pole, and Santa knows it.

One evening Santa and I were having a quiet conversation by the fireplace while Mrs. Santa bustled around fixing us some hot cider and buttered scones. (They were absolutely the very best I've ever tasted!) "She's my best-kept secret," Santa said softly.

"What do you mean, Santa?" I asked

"She literally runs this place," Santa answered. "I'm great at designing and making toys, and I get a real kick out of delivering them around the world. But I'm a lousy organizer. If Mrs. Santa weren't helping me out, I'm afraid not much would get done."

"What about the elves?" I asked.

"Oh, they're horrible!" Santa said. "They like to help out and all, and I've never seen such hard workers anywhere else in the world—but you have to really watch them to keep them on the Christmas schedule. And it's Mrs. Santa who's able to do that.

"But she does so much more than that," he continued. "She takes care of all of us when we're sick. She makes us happy when we're blue. She keeps the whole place clean and livable. She even gives the elf hall a good cleaning after they wake up from their winter's naps."

One of the elves' favorite things is Mrs. Santa reading them a bedtime story. They never seem to get too old for it!

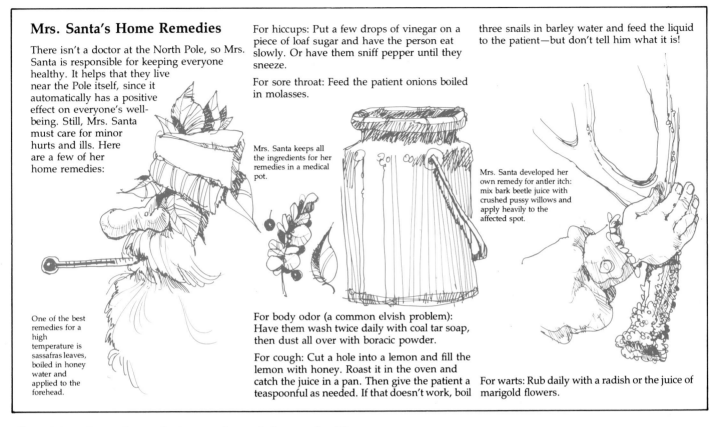

Mrs. Santa's Home Remedies

There isn't a doctor at the North Pole, so Mrs. Santa is responsible for keeping everyone healthy. It helps that they live near the Pole itself, since it automatically has a positive effect on everyone's well-being. Still, Mrs. Santa must care for minor hurts and ills. Here are a few of her home remedies:

One of the best remedies for a high temperature is sassafras leaves, boiled in honey water and applied to the forehead.

For hiccups: Put a few drops of vinegar on a piece of loaf sugar and have the person eat slowly. Or have them sniff pepper until they sneeze.

For sore throat: Feed the patient onions boiled in molasses.

Mrs. Santa keeps all the ingredients for her remedies in a medical pot.

For body odor (a common elvish problem): Have them wash twice daily with coal tar soap, then dust all over with boracic powder.

For cough: Cut a hole into a lemon and fill the lemon with honey. Roast it in the oven and catch the juice in a pan. Then give the patient a teaspoonful as needed. If that doesn't work, boil

three snails in barley water and feed the liquid to the patient—but don't tell him what it is!

Mrs. Santa developed her own remedy for antler itch: mix bark beetle juice with crushed pussy willows and apply heavily to the affected spot.

For warts: Rub daily with a radish or the juice of marigold flowers.

Then Mrs. Santa brought in our late-night snack. "I hear you're pretty important around here," I said. "Sounds like the place would fall apart without you."

Santa grinned broadly, and Mrs. Santa blushed. "You know it's true, Mama," Santa said, and he pulled her down onto his lap. "In fact, she's so vital to my work that if there were no Mrs. Santa, I'm afraid there wouldn't be a Santa either."

He gave his wife a squeeze, then turned to me. "You can write that down in your book, Alden, for all the world to see. Then the secret will be out: There's only one reason why Santa Claus is famous. Because Mrs. Santa helped him get that way."

I was going to ask more questions about it, but I could tell it was a lost cause. With Mrs. Santa on his lap, Santa seemed to have totally forgotten I was even there!

"You know you're loved when Mrs. Santa gives you a hug," Santa said to me. "And I get lots of them!"

Where Mrs. Santa Came From

Anwyn was her name. She was more beautiful than the sparkling sun on white-tipped waves. Her hair was shining gold, as if mined from the rarest lode in the earth. Her eyes were a deep and steady blue, like the sky on a clear summer's day. Her name was Anwyn, and she was a princess.

Her father, the king, was dead. He'd been killed in an avalanche while seeking to rescue some of his subjects who'd been stranded high in a mountain pass. She'd never known her mother. The queen had died in giving Anwyn birth.

A regent had been appointed to rule until Anwyn was of age. He was a clever man, well trained in wiles and trickery. And as Anwyn began to reach the age of queenship, the regent began to lay his evil plans.

In April of that year (the princess would come of age in August), the regent, Vontue, sent out a proclamation. "All people will henceforth become the same," he proclaimed. "Those who are not the same will be cast out—or killed."

It became a revolution. "No more royalty!" the people chanted in the streets. "No more nobility! No rich! No poor! Same! Same! Same!"

Everyone lined up at the barber shops to get the same haircut—just like the regent's. Everyone put in orders at the tailor's to get the same kind of clothes—just like the regent's.

Vontue set his sinister plan into effect by issuing the proclamation.

Princess Anwyn became increasingly isolated. Soon she had only her music, her bif-bif, and her handmaiden to keep her company.

11

Soon everyone looked the same as everyone else. Vontue looked like the people, and the people looked like him. His sinister plan was working.

"This is the most marvelous movement of all ages," the newspapers proclaimed. "The doctrine of sameness is truly inspired, created by genius. It is the liberating force of the masses. It brings down the rich and elevates the poor, bringing an equality that has eluded the human race from the beginning."

Vontue smiled and continued his plotting. The people cheered at the inns and lodging houses; they marched and chanted before the shops.

But beautiful Anwyn did not smile. She didn't cheer. "I *like* being different," she said. "I like being myself." Only her closest handmaiden would listen.

Vontue's pernicious philosophy, as noted in his proclamation, has pervaded much of our modern-day thinking.

The people thronged the streets, shouting out the glories of *sameness!*

"Down with Uppity People!"

"Sameness is Best!"

"Differentness is Worst!"

"Everything and Everyone—the Same!"

Vontue came with the guards and took away all her fine clothes, leaving her only gray, drab ones in exchange. He brought in a barber, who shaved her head. Her long blond tresses fell lifeless onto the floor. "It's wonderful to be the *same*, isn't it!" the barber exclaimed.

In the night Anwyn wrapped a heavy scarf around her head, put the drab clothes on, and, with her handmaiden, fled the palace.

Vontue didn't pursue. Anwyn had done only what he had most wanted.

Anwyn and her maiden made their long and arduous way into the north. It was many days before they were out of the kingdom, away from the threat of the *same*. Finally they arrived in the quiet little village of Stil, nestled peacefully in the mountains. They had no money and no friends. The princess was no longer beautiful, for she wore the heavy scarf over her head to cover her baldness, and her face was etched with lines of care.

After Anwyn's hair was cut, a secret admirer gathered her precious hair and kept it hidden for many years. It's now on display at the Copenhagen Royal Museum.

When Santa met Princess Anwyn, she was serving tables at a wayside inn.

The handmaiden was able to find work doing laundry, but her income was insufficient to support both of them. The princess went to work at an inn, serving the travelers and changing the beds once a week.

She'd been there almost a year when a young man with a kindly face and red cheeks came stomping out of the snow one evening. He took off his red cap and laid it on the counter. He took one look at Anwyn and smiled. Her hair had grown back. Her cares had only made her more beautiful. "What's a nice girl like you doing in a place like this?" he asked.

Santa was enchanted by Anwyn's deep blue eyes. She was intrigued by his fresh, thick beard.

And when Santa left on his dogsled a week later, his new wife, Anwyn, and her ever-faithful handmaiden went with him.

After their wedding, Santa put Princess Anwyn on his dogsled and took her north with him.

Note: Many have wondered whatever happened to Princess Anwyn's handmaiden. After serving Anwyn faithfully for many years, the handmaiden, Priscilla, fell in love with a traveling salesman (Max) and emigrated with him to what is now Indiana. They had many children, and their children had children. Their eighteenth great-grandson distinguished himself by serving as a Cabinet member during the Truman administration. And a great-great-great-granddaughter became known as the first woman ever to sing "Stranger's Lullaby" while gargling with a glass of water.

14

Santa's Favorite Treat

Anybody can tell just by looking that Santa loves to eat! He loves food in all its forms: meats, vegetables, pastas, pastries, creams, sauces, drinks, and on and on. He never tires of eating, although somehow he's able to keep his weight down to a pleasant plumpness.

But out of all the foods available to man, there's one treat he likes above all others: the cookie. He's always more than pleased when he finds a cookie (with milk) waiting for him when he drops down a chimney into a home. And he gets pleased beyond all expression when it's his *favorite kind of cookie*—the kind Mrs. Santa makes!

If you want to make Santa happy, leave him some cookies and milk to munch on when he visits your house. And if you want to make him *really* happy, put out his favorite kind!

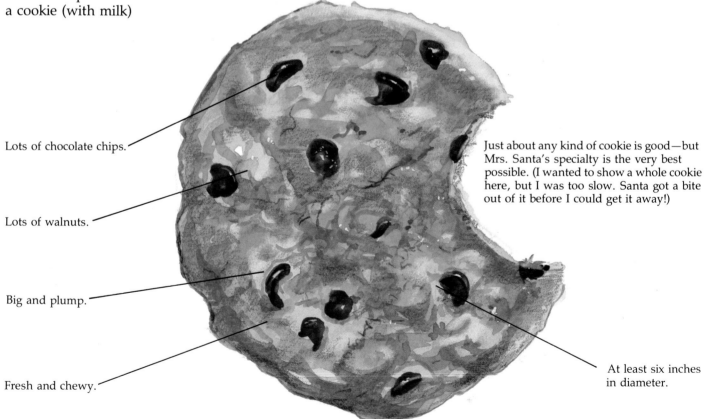

Lots of chocolate chips.

Lots of walnuts.

Big and plump.

Fresh and chewy.

Just about any kind of cookie is good—but Mrs. Santa's specialty is the very best possible. (I wanted to show a whole cookie here, but I was too slow. Santa got a bite out of it before I could get it away!)

At least six inches in diameter.

Take a little cookie,
Try a little taste,
Nibble, nibble, nibble,
Never any waste.
Tastes very good,
Yummy, yummy, yummy,
Eat it all gone,
Fills up your tummy.

Take another cookie . . .

Santa always likes to have a big batch of
his favorite cookies on hand.

Mrs. Santa puts her cookies in the world's largest
cookie jar, which was designed especially for Santa.
He likes to munch on them while he reads on quiet
evenings. He can go through all the cookies in the jar
(approx. 1,029) in less than a week!

Mrs. Santa's Oatmeal Chocolate Chip Nut Cookies

Beat together until smooth:

¾ cup cooking oil (or seal-skin oil, if you can)
½ cup granulated sugar (or glacier sand, if possible)
½ cup brown sugar (or toasted snow flakes)
2 eggs (nerd eggs, if you can find any)

Mix in the following:

2 cups flour (or petals from honey flowers)
½ teaspoon nutmeg (or dried dandelion juice)
½ teaspoon salt (or North Pole ice crystals)
1 teaspoon soda (or ju-ju plant powder, if you can get it)
2 teaspoons cinnamon (or Cimarron sneezes)
1 teaspoon baking powder (or petrified tree sap)
2 cups oatmeal (or uncooked elf mush, if you can buy it)

Mix well, then add 12 ounces of chocolate chips and 1½ cups
of chopped walnuts. Bake at 375 degrees for 13 minutes. Will
give you about three dozen cookies, or one real big one.

17

How Santa Invented Toys

Santa began as a carpenter. He was good at all kinds of woodworking—carving, fitting, joining, shaping, forming. It wasn't long before the things he made were in demand far and wide.

His cabinets were roomy, yet compact. They hung very solidly, and the doors didn't squeak when they were opened.

His chairs were extremely comfortable, being carefully crafted to fit the human body. Some Claus rocking chairs still exist, and are much in demand among antique collectors—though they're next to impossible to find. Most people who have a Claus chair think they just have an old chair their great-grandmother handed down.

Probably most famous was the Santa bed. Santa carved all kinds of intricate scrollwork on the headboard; he made matching nightstands to go on the side. Since Santa likes to read, he also put a place for books on the headboard, which was an innovation—one that caught on among other carpenters.

Because Santa did such excellent work, he was always busy making one thing or another. One day he got in an order from the King: make 64 chairs for the King's

When Santa was young, he was one of the finest carpenters in all the land.

dining room. Santa was delighted. The King always paid well and was willing to pay for the best in materials.

Santa collected the wood and other supplies he needed and got to work. One by one he fashioned the King's dining chairs, working quickly so they'd be ready for a big banquet that was coming up.

But, to his horror, Santa discovered after he'd built 63 chairs that he didn't have enough material to build the sixty-fourth.

"What am I going to do now?" he muttered. "The King ordered sixty-*four*, not *three*." The King wasn't mean or anything—he wasn't going to take Santa's head off. But the guillotine *had* been rather busy lately.

That afternoon Santa went into the forest and talked to all the woodsmen he could find. "I've got to have the same wood I had before," he told them.

One by one the woodsmen turned him down. "We can't get that kind of wood," they said. "It's hard to find and even harder to cut." The sun went low in the sky and it was begining to grow dark. Santa finally turned his back on the woodsmen and began to trudge home.

But just on the edge of the woods he came across a little hut set back among the trees. "I wonder . . . ," Santa murmured to himself, and he went to the door and knocked.

A bent old man came to the door.

"Are you a woodsman?" Santa asked.

The old man shook his head. "I'm the tender of the trees," he said. "I'm their shepherd."

Santa looked at him carefully. "Then you know where each kind of wood can be found, don't you. And you know how to cut it."

The old man smiled. "There's nothing about the forest that I don't know."

Then it was Santa's turn to smile. "I desperately need your help," Santa said. And he explained his problem.

The old man was reluctant. He didn't like to cut his trees. But he finally agreed to see if he could find one that had fallen—Santa didn't want a green tree anyway.

19

"But it will be at least a day before I can get it to you," the old man warned.

"That's all right," Santa said. "If you can get it to me by tomorrow night, I'll still be able to make the chair in time."

The next morning Santa stewed all day. What if the tender of the trees couldn't find the right wood? The King wasn't cruel—but he *had* destroyed three villages for not including enough cream in the milk they sent for taxes.

That night the moon had risen high before the knock came at Santa's door. Santa rushed to open it. There stood the tender of the trees. His hands were empty. . . .

Santa went right to bed, worried about what he'd do. In the night he had a dream. He dreamed that the King was good and kind and generous and loving. And that he cut off the hands of those who didn't make enough chairs for him.

In the morning Santa went out to his shop. There at one end were 63 chairs, carefully stacked and ready for delivery. There on the workbench were a few scraps of wood left. *What can a man do with those?* he thought.

Suddenly, on impulse, he picked up the wood. He ran his fingers down the grain. It was such fine wood, smooth to the touch.

"The King ordered 64 chairs," he said to himself. "I'll make him 64 chairs."

He grasped his knife and began to carve.

By the end of the day, Santa had finished his creation—a little chair about as high as a unicorn horn. It was an exact duplicate of the big chairs he'd made for the King.

But as he stared at it, he thought it looked kind of forlorn there, all empty and quiet. No one would ever sit in it, because no one was that size. It was kind of sad.

Santa picked up the last scrap of wood he had left, looking at it carefully. If there was no one who could fit in the chair, Santa would *make* someone! He carved into the night, not even stopping for supper. Finally, just before midnight, he stopped. In his hand was a perfect little girl. He held her against the candle light for a moment, then sat her in the chair. It was just the right size.

Santa tossed and turned all night, with bad dreams about what the King was going to do to him.

20

There was one small scrap of wood left. Suddenly Santa got a brilliant idea.

The next day Santa loaded all the chairs onto a big cart and hauled them over to the palace. He took them into the banquet room and set them up around the huge table. At one end he put the tiny chair with the tiny girl in it.

Then he fetched the King. "Sire," he said, "I've made you my finest chairs."

The King smiled broadly. "These are fine chairs, indeed!" he exclaimed. He walked with Santa around the long table, looking at the chairs, running his fingers over the exquisite wood—and counting. Finally they got to the end. The King was smiling no longer. "I ordered 64 chairs," he said, and his voice was very, very quiet. "And you brought only 63."

Santa started to answer, but the King interrupted him. 'I'm a very patient man," he said. "I'm easy to please." He stopped and stroked his beard. "You'll remember the people of Remikin Valley, of course. They tried to sell me blind cows. They've found it rather difficult to herd cattle with no feet to walk on!" He laughed imperiously.

The chair looked lonely and forlorn, until Santa made a little girl to sit in it.

Note: The little girl Santa made to put in the little chair was the first doll ever made—in fact, it was the first toy of any kind! (For more information, see *Where Toys Came From,* Marx Kenner Mattel III, New York: John Boswell Publishing, 1909.)

The King was furious when he saw
there were only 63 big chairs—and
one little one.

"I ordered 64 chairs," the King repeated. "Big ones.
None like *this!*" He pointed at the little chair Santa had
made.

Santa started to answer, but just then the little
Princess, Anwyn, came running into the banquet
room. "Daddy," she began, but then she stopped
herself. She looked at the tiny chair with the tiny girl
in it. She'd never seen anything like it before. She
looked closely, picked up the girl, stroked its carved
head.

Then she stared up at the King, her big blue eyes
luminous. "Daddy! A chair just for me!" Her mouth
split wide in a smile.

The King looked at her, not blinking. "It's wonderful!"
the Princess said. She giggled and bent beside the
chair to play with the wooden girl.

The King smiled at her, despite himself. "It *is* a rather
remarkable thing," he said.

Santa sighed and took a deep breath.

"I'm going to name her," the Princess said. "I'll call
her Dolly."

Thus was the first toy created.

When Princess Anwyn saw the little
chair, with the little girl sitting in it,
she was delighted.

Note: As an interesting footnote to this story, the Princess Anwyn who got the first toy ever made was
the same Princess Anwyn who later married Santa Claus. See "Where Mrs. Santa Came From."

Santa's Favorite Song

Santa loves to sing. He has a wonderfully mellow baritone voice, and it's a pleasure to hear it. He enjoys hearing it himself, and he's always surprised at its quality. He's quite modest about his voice, almost as if it were someone else entirely that he was listening to.

When Santa was growing up, he became quite proficient on the harp and the lute. Using those instruments, he would entertain those around him, lifting their spirits and making the world seem more joyful.

Or he could sing a sad song, leaving everyone in his audience sobbing huge tears.

Over the years Santa has learned literally thousands of songs. He'll belt them out without notice or provocation, singing "Hey-Hi-Ho-Ho-Ho!" which is a lively, bouncy little tune; or maybe he'll sing "The Night of the Sad, Sad Sadness," which will make one weep.

But Santa's favorite song is one he wrote himself. It's called "It's Christmas All the Year," and it's his message to people everywhere. (It's reproduced in his own handwriting on the next page.) "I love everybody," he said to me. "When we can learn to sing together, and to dance as loving partners, we'll finally find the happiness we're all seeking so desperately."

When Santa sings his favorite song he always gets a little emotional.

24

It's Christmas All the Year

Sometimes Santa sings two other verses of the song. They follow the first verse and are sung with the same notes:

I'm Santa Claus, the Christmas man;/I clasp my hands with others./When we all love, we're family;/We're sisters and we're brothers. (Repeat chorus.)

I'm Santa Claus, a friend of elves;/I joy to see life's sharing./When people love the whole year through,/We all grow from the caring. (Repeat chorus.)

Why Santa Likes You

I had the opportunity to sit with Santa one day as he opened his mail. As he opened letter after letter, I found myself growing more and more amazed. He knew every one of them! He knows—and loves—every child in the world. Even when they're naughty!

For instance, there was little Carlos Medina in Mexico City. "Carlos helps his mother whenever he gets a chance," Santa said. "He's a great kid!"

Then Santa opened a letter from a girl name Claudine, who lives in Quebec. "This Claudine," Santa said, tapping the letter in his hand. "She's really something. She doesn't have any legs. But she sure has a big smile!"

Next on the stack was a note from John Parry, a boy from Wales. "John is one of the best soccer players in the world," Santa said. "He runs well and kicks well. And most important of all, he's a good sport!"

Why does Santa like you? Because you're special. There's no one else in the whole world who's quite the way you are. And that makes you pretty neat!

"I never met a kid I didn't like."
Santa Claus

26

Santa's Garden

When spring first breaks, Santa rushes out into his garden, whooping in excitement. Finally he's free of being cooped up! His garden isn't a large lot—only 100 feet long by 40 feet wide. "But it keeps the cobwebs out of my head," Santa chuckles.

The days are so long during the North Pole's summer that Santa can grow almost anything he wants. And the growth rate of his plants is truly incredible. For instance, his rutabagas are ready to harvest only 27 days after planting. And eggplants take only 22 days to mature. Some seasons Santa is able to get over half a dozen plantings of certain vegetables.

Mrs. Santa is in charge of planting flowers around the house. Her specialties are tulips, which come back every year, and orchids, which she has to grow around the house. (One year some young reindeer got into her flowers and had a feast. If you think Mrs. Santa doesn't ever get mad, you didn't see her that day!)

Santa never uses bug spray in his garden—he simply instructs the insects to stay out. And they do!

Horticultural Experimentation. The plants in Santa's gardens grow so fast, once summer gets rolling, that he's able to do some interesting experiments in grafting and cross-mixing. He can take a new creation through several generations of refinement and have a whole new, perfect vegetable or fruit at the end of just one summer.

If he and Mrs. Santa really like the new plant, he'll keep the seeds for the following year. But some aren't such a big hit—those he'll discard, in hopes everyone will forget the horrible taste.

Some of Santa's successful combinations:

the apple-nut tree (shown below)

the parrot, created by combining a pea plant with a carrot*

the born, which has beans growing on a corn cob

the cantamelon, a watermelon-sized cantaloupe

the lima-pea (shown below)

Some of Santa's bright ideas that turned out rather dull:

the stewberry, a berry designed to taste like little pieces of meat, to put in stews

the potomato, a combination of potato and tomato which was red and tasted like a squishy potato

the squashaloupe, Santa's attempt to make the cantaloupe the size and shape of a banana squash (Mrs. Santa's response: "It's the right color, but it tastes like wood!")

Mrs. Santa's Creation

After the harvest is in, Mrs. Santa gets to work in her kitchen, bottling things for the long winter. She loves to experiment with fancy combinations—and she hasn't failed yet to make everything tasty.

Mrs. Santa's Carrot and Pea Jam is a favorite of the elves. It tastes best when made from the parrot plant.

Here's her recipe:

First, gather about a pound of parrots. Steam them in a covered pan.

Second, get four cups of gooseberries. Mix with three cups of sugar.

Third, cut two small apples (without cores) into small pieces and mix with the gooseberries.

Fourth, simmer the berry mixture until it reaches the desired thickness.

Fifth, take the parrots off the stove, add butter, salt, and pepper, and eat.

Sixth, now that you're not so hungry anymore, take the berry mixture off the stove and pour into bottles. It will store through the winter.

*Author's Note: I've tasted this strange vegetable (the parrot). It grows in a pod, and is truly a work of horticultural art. All the vegetables within the pod are round, but every other one is green, while the others are orangish. Oddly enough, the green pieces taste like carrots; the orange pieces taste like peas. The vegetable is delicious whether eaten raw or cooked.

The apple-nut tree produces apples and walnuts simultaneously, though never on the same branch.

The lima-pea plant is a successful cross between a lima bean and a green pea.

Santa's prize-winning butternut squash consistently wins grand prizes at the Lapland Autumn Fair. (Note the small seed cavity—it provides enough seeds for propagation, and leaves more room for the meat!)

Santa's Favorite Jokes

Santa loves a good joke. He must—he tells the same ones over and over again, time after time! Here are some of his favorites:

I just got back from my yearly flight around the world. Boy, are my arms tired! . . . After I left home, I wrote my mother that I'd grown another foot. So she knit me another sock.

Let me tell you about the Ice Nymphs. Once three nymphs were sleeping in the same bed. It was so crowded that one got out and slept on the floor. After a while, one of the Nymphs said to the one on the floor, "You ought to get back in the bed with us. There's lots more room now!" . . . Once the Nymphs were out playing football. One of the players asked the coach to flood the field so he could go in as a sub.

Then there are the elves. One of the elves is great at magic. He walked around the corner and turned into an outhouse. . . . One elf snored so loud he woke himself up. But then he solved the problem—he started sleeping in the next room. . . . Everyone knows that elves are famous for the baths they take each year. But perhaps you don't know what the first elf in the tub is called—he's the ringleader. . . . We've got one elf who just hates to take baths. Once he got so dirty that when he finally took a bath he found some underwear he thought he'd lost three years before.

With all my expertise over the years I've learned some interesting things. For instance, if a bee and a doorbell get married, what kind of children do you think they'll have? Humdingers! . . . And I've learned why penguins cross the road only halfway—they like to lay it on the line. . . . I deliver toys to a boy who parts his hair from ear to ear. Its a real problem—people keep whispering in his nose!

People always have questions about my reindeer. For instance, they want to know why reindeer wear bells. I tell them it's because their horns don't work. . . . Or they ask, "How much reindeer feed do you get for a quarter?" My answer: "None. Quarters don't eat reindeer feed!"

Santa always loves a good laugh. If no one else will give him one, he'll give it to himself!

29

Why Santa Says "Ho! Ho! Ho!"

In ancient China, Master Ho was the supreme artist of the martial arts. Over many years he perfected his skill, physically, intellectually, and . . . vocally. Master Ho became so skilled with the use of his voice that he developed the ability simply to speak his name in a humorous way and his opponent would fall over laughing. Then Ho could do as he wished with the enemy. It was the pinnacle of the art.

The opponent would attack. Ho would step back, without even raising his hands, "Ho! Ho!" he'd say.

The opponent would fall back, disarmed and smiling. "Ho! Ho! Ho!" Ho would say. The opponent would bend over, convulsed in laughter. Ho would step forward, touch his enemy on the neck with a slight pressure, and the man would fall over dead.

In his many studies Santa learned about Master Ho. Chinese history leaves a complete record of Ho's

Santa has earned a red belt in Ho Karate—and more than once he's had to use his *Ho*ing skill to resist the attack of bullies. With a double dose of triple *Ho*s, the bullies are rolling in laughter long after Santa is gone.

techniques—and Santa decided to try them. His purpose, though, wasn't to overwhelm and kill. Instead he hoped simply to master the art of making people laugh.

Santa practiced for many years, gradually gaining more and more skill with Ho Karate. He practiced on Mrs. Claus; he practiced on the elves. Finally he felt he was ready to try it on an outsider. He crept down a chimney in Liverpool, England, and found he was face to face with a befuddled homeowner.

"What in the world—" the homeowner started.

"Ho! Ho!" Santa said, and the homeowner smiled. "Ho! Ho! Ho!" and the homeowner started to laugh out loud.

Fake Santas can say "Ho! Ho! Ho!" with no effect whatsoever. But when Santa says it, people laugh! They can't help themselves. They laugh until the tears roll out of their eyes. They laugh in guffaws and chuckles and giggles. Their eyes squeeze together; their lips turn up; their cheeks push up ever-so-slightly; their mouths open wide—and there it comes!

Proper Usage of "Ho! Ho! Ho!"

"Ho!" alone has little power. It can be effective for getting started, however. Once one "Ho!" has been sounded, it's difficult to prevent another from rolling across the lips. One "Ho!" is also used to alert the listener that the "Ho! Ho! Ho!" is about to be sounded.

"Ho! Ho!" is effective in creating a smile. The sound is so inherently mirthful that the listener smiles just in hearing it—just as the reader is now smiling in thinking of that delectable sound of "Ho! Ho!" "Ho! Ho!" is rarely used without going to the third step of *Ho*s, though the speaker with great self-control *can* limit himself only to two *Ho*s.

"Ho! Ho! Ho!" is the zenith of the art. If said correctly, it gives the speaker overwhelming power over the listener. Each *aitch* should be carefully aspirated; each *oh* should be spoken clearly, but cut off short. *Oh*s that are drawn out lose their punch. Once a single set of "Ho! Ho! Ho!" has been pronounced, a second should not be spoken to that listener for quite some time, or his body will grow unbearably weak from the release of joyous energy.

"Ho! Ho! Ho! Ho!" is overdoing the whole thing, and should be totally avoided. Those who sink so low as to speak four *Ho*s in succession have no right to the art at all.

Warning: Don't try the powerful "Ho! Ho! Ho!" on Santa. You may have some innate abilities with the art, and Santa may fall down in laughter, making him late for the rest of his rounds.

The Magical Pomegranate

In the land north of the North Pole stands the Magical Pomegranate Tree. It's a tall and beautiful tree, with branches arching over a wide meadow. The leaves sparkle in the sunlight; and the branches of the tree glisten in the moonlight.

More than one traveler has been dazzled and entranced by the splendor of the Magical Pomegranate Tree—and as he thus stood in the tree's spell, the Polar Dragon swooped down and cooked him to a crisp with his supremely hot breath!

After Santa moved to the North Pole, he was always cold. He shivered and shivered, and could never get warm.

The Polar Dragon was always intensely jealous of the Magical Pomegranate Tree, and he guarded it constantly. For the tree bears fruit, one solitary pomegranate, only once every thousand years. And the dragon always wanted to be certain the fruit would be *his!*

But all this was before Santa Claus.

Many, many centuries ago, Santa learned of the Magical Pomegranate Tree. It was said that the fruit would make one warm—one tiny seed from the pomegranate would make the eater warm for many years after.

Santa stroked his beard—and shivered under his coat—when he heard tell of the tree. "My, my," he said to Mrs. Santa, "Imagine never being cold up here again!"

Mrs. Santa smiled sadly as she heated bricks to put under the foot of their bed. "Don't even think it, Santa. It's only a dream."

But the idea of the Magical Pomegranate Tree preyed on Santa's mind, and every time he had a moment free from designing or making gifts, he thought of the pomegranate that was supposed to make a person warm.

"It's supposed to bear fruit right in the middle of our millennium," he said idly to Mrs. Santa one night. "That's next year. . . ."

Mrs. Santa shook her head. "Don't worry your head about it, dear. If the tree does exist, then I'm sure the Polar Dragon does too. And I'm not real anxious for you to go tromping around where dragons fly!"

Santa wasn't listening. He was too busy rubbing his half-frozen toes.

Christmas came and went, and Santa caught a terrific cold making his rounds. "It's the blasted wind-chill factor," he complained. "It gets me every year!"

The spring dawned. One morning Santa jumped out of bed and made an announcement: "I'm going after the magical pomegranate." Mrs Santa tried to talk him out of it, but it was no use. His mind was made up.

The journey to the land north of the North Pole wasn't far, but it was hard. And with every step Santa took, he got colder and colder. He pulled his hood close around his cheeks. He put gloves over his gloves. He put insulated boots over his boots. And still he froze from the biting wind and heartless ice of the land north of the North Pole.

One day Santa topped a rise and looked down into a broad valley. There, glistening brightly in the very center of the valley, was a tall tree with reddish bark. "The Magical Pomegranate Tree!" he whispered. He stumbled down the hill and into the valley. "Warmth! Warmth!"

But just as he reached the valley floor he heard a tremendous roar above him. The sky darkened. The air crashed as with thunder. Santa put his hands on his ears and fell to the snowy ground. The Polar Dragon swooped down, claws outstretched—but at the last minute Santa rolled out of reach. The dragon growled deep in his throat, then smashed into the snow a few feet away. Then he turned and faced Santa. "Who are you that comes into my valley?"

Santa started to stutter out an answer, but he couldn't think. All he was aware of was those evil eyes, which held him in their spell. The dragon flicked out his long tongue, then growled again. "So you think you could come in here and steal my fruit, do you? I've been guarding it for 999 years now—and, as you might imagine, I'm very hungry!"

The dragon took a step forward, still holding Santa in his gaze. "You're pretty small," the dragon said, "but small is better than no dinner at all. I haven't had dinner for six years now."

Santa stared, eyes wide. The dragon took another step. He breathed down into Santa's face—and the stench of his breath broke the spell. Santa tore his eyes away and looked at the ground. "I didn't come to steal your fruit," Santa said. "I came to tell you of a great treasure I found. Not far from here."

The dragon stopped, interested. Everyone knows that dragons are fools for treasures and jewels, and Santa knew it too.

"Why would you tell me about it?" the dragon asked, his voice suddenly soft. "Why not just keep it all for yourself—and not risk your life?"

Santa sighed, pretending to be very tired. "I couldn't carry much of it. And your back is so broad, and your wings so strong. I thought I'd give you most of it, if you would help me carry mine home."

"Well, now," the dragon said. "Well, now." He stopped and stared into the distance. "And where be this great treasure?"

Santa raised his head, and pointed to the south. "That way, where the sun meets the mountain. Under the stream that falls. Between the two tallest trees."

The dragon chuckled slow and low. His belly rippled with the sound. "Yesssss," he said, his tongue darting out and his eyes half-closing. "Under the stream that falls. Well, we'll see about this." And with a jerk he was into the air and gone.

Santa stood and raced down the valley to where the tree stood. He knew he didn't have much time. The mountains were far away—but dragons can go very fast. Santa ran until his sides hurt. The breath pushed in and out of him with great heaving effort. Finally he reached the tree. It was too beautiful to touch. He stared at it, breathing hard, his eyes aching from the wonder of it all.

Then he remembered the dragon and quickly plucked the magical pomegranate from its stem on the tree. The tree seemed to stand up taller; its golden leaves blazed brighter in the sun.

In the same instant, the sky grew dark, and Santa heard a hoarse roar above him. "Humannnn!" the voice said, biting down to the very core of Santa's being. "Humannnnnn!"

Santa tucked the fruit inside his coat and began to run. He ran across the valley and back up the hill. The dragon ran behind him, laughing, toying with him as a cat would with a mouse.

"You tricked me, my pretty," the dragon laughed. "But no matter! I'll still have you—*and* the fruit!"

Santa ran as far as he could, then ran farther. Finally, exhausted, he fell face-forward into the snow. *This is it,* he thought. *I've lived so long, but now it's over.*

He lay still, waiting for the hot blast of flame that would surely issue from the dragon's foul mouth.

But it didn't come. He waited some more—and still it didn't come. Then he heard a quiet sobbing behind him. He sat up and turned around. The Polar Dragon sat back on his haunches, great tears streaming from his eyes. He looked down at Santa. "I tried to roast you," he said, his voice choking. "But you've stolen my magic. No fire would come out. Watch!" And he belched forth at Santa. Only smoke and stink came out.

Santa smiled grimly up at the dragon. "So you've done your last dirty deed," he said. "Well, come along with me, and I'll take care of you. But no pomegranates! Then your fire will come back and I don't doubt for a minute that you'd cook me for supper!"

So Santa took the magical pomegranate fruit home with him, and the Polar Dragon followed behind.

"Give me your word of honor that you won't eat any seeds, and I'll let you guard the pomegranate," Santa said to the dragon. He knew that once a dragon promises, he will always do what he says.

"I give my word of honor," the dragon said. But he didn't look very happy about it.

Still, he had agreed. Now the dragon guards the magical pomegranate faithfully. And now Santa eats one seed of the fruit every fifty years, and Mrs. Santa takes one too. It makes them feel wonderful inside—and they haven't been cold since!

The seeds of the magical pomegranate work to make Santa warm. He only has to take one every fifty years.

When the dragon saw Santa taking the magical pomegranate, he grew absolutely furious.

34

Santa's Inventions

Raful, the elf, was the model when Santa carved the Gramophone.

Ever since he was a little boy, Santa has loved to invent things. Whenever he has a chance, he goes into his shop and just tinkers around. Most of his inventions are toys, but he also invents things that really benefit mankind, such as the toothpick and the baby rattle.

GRAMOPHONE

The movable lens on the telescope can rotate more than 180 degrees.

The gearing used on the rotation device was a refinement suggested by Mrs. Santa.

The Gramophone

The Gramophone plays over 5,000 tunes. When you wind it up, the elf sings the songs.

World's Largest Telescope

Santa telescope, the most powerful in the world, is designed to see around the curvature of the earth. Santa's even seen himself in it! The telescope can also see through walls. Santa invented it to show him if boys and girls around the world are being naughty or nice.

An exciting feature of the telescope is the receiving antenna, which can pick up voices from anywhere in the world.

Source:

—Santa Claus, *Invention Sketchbook*, unpublished, North Pole Archives.

—Personal patent search, November 12 and 13, 1981, U. S. Bureau of Patents, Washington, D. C.

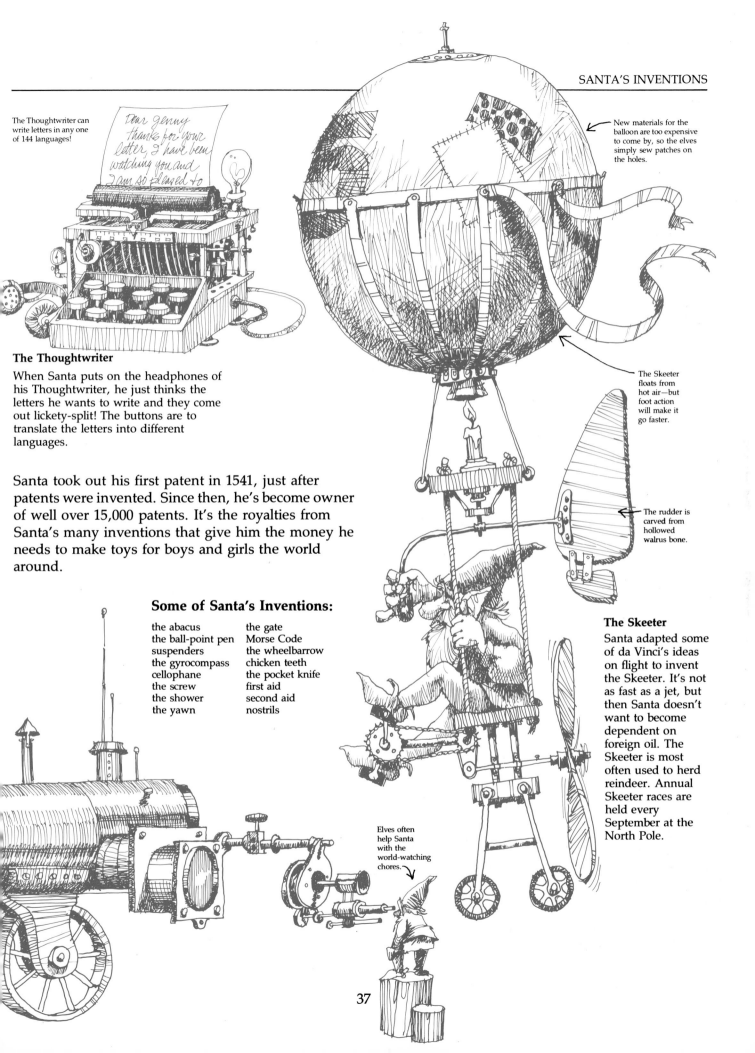

The Thoughtwriter can write letters in any one of 144 languages!

New materials for the balloon are too expensive to come by, so the elves simply sew patches on the holes.

The Thoughtwriter

When Santa puts on the headphones of his Thoughtwriter, he just thinks the letters he wants to write and they come out lickety-split! The buttons are to translate the letters into different languages.

Santa took out his first patent in 1541, just after patents were invented. Since then, he's become owner of well over 15,000 patents. It's the royalties from Santa's many inventions that give him the money he needs to make toys for boys and girls the world around.

The Skeeter floats from hot air—but foot action will make it go faster.

The rudder is carved from hollowed walrus bone.

Some of Santa's Inventions:

the abacus	the gate
the ball-point pen	Morse Code
suspenders	the wheelbarrow
the gyrocompass	chicken teeth
cellophane	the pocket knife
the screw	first aid
the shower	second aid
the yawn	nostrils

The Skeeter

Santa adapted some of da Vinci's ideas on flight to invent the Skeeter. It's not as fast as a jet, but then Santa doesn't want to become dependent on foreign oil. The Skeeter is most often used to herd reindeer. Annual Skeeter races are held every September at the North Pole.

Elves often help Santa with the world-watching chores.

37

Why Santa
Lives So Long

Here is a great mystery, fully understood by few. Yet it's so important to Santa's survival that a clear explanation must be made.

Santa is the oldest man on earth. No one's sure how old he really is, and he isn't giving out the information. Perhaps even Santa doesn't know how old he is.

It doesn't hurt that Santa was born with some elf-blood in him. Elves live incredibly long times, and Santa benefited from that tendency to longevity. But in many ways he was like a normal man before he moved to the North Pole. That's when the magic really began.

Positive thought ions are among the most powerful energy sources known to man.

The North Pole's powerful magnetism pulls all positive thought ions up to the north, lengthening Santa's life.

Some people send (or sent) out such powerful positive thought ions that they have become famous for it. Here are some of their names:
Albert Schweitzer
Mother Theresa
Norman Vincent Peale
John Davidson
Richard the Lionhearted
King Arthur
Robin Hood
Cock Robin

What kids look like when they believe in Santa and send out positive thought ions.

Deep in the crust of the earth, centered right at the North Pole, is a mass of magnetic rock that collects positive ions from around the world. (A simple experiment will demonstrate this to anyone: The metal in the compass is made from positive metal ions. Hold the compass in your hand and see where it points. Right at the North Pole! The magnetic rock is pulling at the ions!) When Santa moved to the North Pole, he discovered the magnetic rock. But he knew it worked inefficiently, especially in the collection of positive *thought* ions.

So Santa developed a special pole, made of wood and metal and magic, that would provide a focus for the rock's energies. The pole and the rock, working together, pull in positive thought ions from all around the world. Those ions collect within the rock and benefit everyone who's near them.

(In preparing materials for this book, I spent over a year at the North Pole. When I arrived there, I looked at least 45 years old. When I returned to my home in the United States, I looked no more than 30.)

Those positive thought ions are a direct cause for Santa's being able to live so long. They invigorate and rejuvenate him. They take the worry wrinkles from his eyes and replace them with laugh lines. They give his hands new strength. They make his muscles powerful. Mrs. Santa swears that every year they live at the North Pole they both get younger!

No one sends positive thought ions on purpose. When people laugh or smile or talk happily, the positive thought ions automatically exude from them. When they frown or fight, negative thought ions are sent out.

Negative thought ions are bad for Santa. But positive thought ions are wonderful.

How does Santa live so long? Because we think good things. If we stopped being happy, Santa would die.

IT ALL DEPENDS ON YOU!

Sending out positive thought ions isn't difficult. All it requires is a little faith and a lot of happiness!

39

Santa's Clothes

Prior to the 1680s, Santa wore anything that was warm. Some years his clothes were made up of reindeer hair and were brown; some years he wore cotton and wool, and his clothes were white.

But early in the 1680s, Santa realized he needed a trademark, so people would know it was him coming down their chimney, and not some robber. Since that time he's worn the same clothes every year—though he usually reserves the red overcoat and the red hat for his Christmas rounds.

As might be imagined, Mrs. Santa has a real laundering chore when Santa gets back from his Christmas rounds. Each chimney he goes down makes him progressively dirtier, though his outer clothes are specially designed to absorb soot so he doesn't track it all over everybody's houses. But by the time he's done his clothes are filled in every thread and seam and fiber.

Mrs. Claus cleans the clothes using a very simple, though effective, method: she lays them outside and lets the snow build up on them. By the spring thaw (such as there is at the North Pole), the clothes are fresh and clean again, ready to wear!

Santa's Special Vest

All of Santa's clothing is special, but his vest is particularly so. He acquired his vest long before any other part of his outfit, and it's the only article of clothing that he hasn't needed to replace.

Long ago, when Santa was still young, he was able to do a great favor for a group of tribesmen in Afghanistan. He literally saved their necks—and in gratitude they gave him a magic vest. "Keep this vest close to your heart forever," they told him, "and it will serve you well."

Their promise has been fulfilled many times over. As the years have passed, Santa has discovered all kinds of uses for his magic vest. For example, it protects him against flying birds (even big ones) and violent clouds. And recently he's discovered a particularly nice feature of the vest's pockets. Although they look small, for some reason they'll hold a great deal of stuff.

He puts them to good use. As he makes his Christmas rounds he is given thousands of cookies and glasses of milk. It's too much for even Santa to eat, but he can't refuse the gift. So he takes it all with him. Into one vest pocket goes all the cookies. Into the other goes the milk. After he gets home, and after the elves wake up from their winter's nap, they enjoy cookies and milk through the whole summer! All because of the Afghan vest!

(Santa allowed me to take a fiber from the vest to analyze. Tests reveal that it was made of rare Afghan Zhubhjnky fish fur.)

Note: Compare these clothes with the clothes worn by the Faker, which are often made of Dacron or nylon or even polyester. And many Fake Santas don't even wear a shirt under their outer coat! Check it—you'll see for yourself!

On anyone else, Santa's outfit would make the person look really silly. But Santa isn't just anyone—he's made the wardrobe into a symbol of happiness.

Santa's red hat with white trim and white ball. The ball is not simply decorative, but helps keep Santa's neck warm.

The coat, fur-lined inside. Santa explains he wears red "because it keeps the flies and mosquitoes off. They don't like red." (Try it—it works!)

The trousers are soft leather and come from the Red Wooger. They are waterproof, which is an urgent necessity when you're flying around outside in the winter. The suspenders are more than for show, since Santa often foregoes the belt when he's not dressing formally.

Santa's first shirt, worn in warmer weather. When the weather is colder, Santa combines this shirt with a second one exactly like it.

The belt, made in the USA and donated by Smith Bros. Beltworks. Santa has worn the same belt for 129 Christmases now.

Santa's underwear is made of elf hair. It took many seasons of haircuts to collect enough of the hair—but it was worth it. The union suit he wears is extremely durable and very warm.

Santa's socks are made of virgin wool from sheep raised in Argentina. Note how both toe and heel are reinforced.

The boots, fur-lined. In very cold weather Santa can fold the top of the boots up over his calves to keep his legs warmer.

Source:
—For more details on Santa's wardrobe, see *Gentleman's Quarterly*, Winter 1932, pp. 110-14. Also see *Vogue*, December 1955, pp. 36-42.

The Christmas Schedule

DEC 24

Without a doubt, Christmas is the most exciting time of the year up at the North Pole. It sets your heart to pounding; it gets the blood flowing; it sends the adrenaline pumping through your veins.

There's so much to do when Christmas Eve comes that Santa has to have a set schedule—otherwise he'd never get off on time. Of course, Santa's on a schedule long before that. As Santa's daddy always used to say, "Prior planning prevents poor presents." Santa has lived by that saying all his life.

But the rush is really on once delivery day arrives. Here's the schedule Santa follows beginning the day before Christmas:

Santa's boots are all shined and ready to go before he even gets up.

Because Santa is going to be up all the next night, he sleeps in a little late the day before Christmas. But not too late. About 7:30 a.m. he's up and getting ready. He bathes, shaves, dresses—and tries to wake up!

42

His first priority of the day is to get the list from Robert, the telephone mouse. He reviews the list while he eats his breakfast. Robert has arranged the list by country and city. Santa memorizes the main points. But he'll take the list with him to help him with the details.

The elves help Santa go over the Christmas list for a last-minute check.

By the day before Christmas, the sleigh is already all loaded and ready. But still Santa needs to check it all out. He checks the toys in the bag, to make sure they're packed tightly. He makes sure they're arranged according to city and country, to match Mouse Robert's list. He double-checks the reins, to be certain they're not going to chafe the reindeer.

The reins are vital to a successful Christmas trip—the elves make sure they have no kinks or nicks in them.

Finally he's ready to take off. He leaves in the early afternoon and flies all the way to the other side of the world, to the South Pole. He starts delivering toys there first, then works his way north and west as the night progresses. One thing that helps him do the whole job in one night is the time difference from place to place. He can start delivering in Australia and the Philippines, after the kids are in bed on Christmas Eve—and it's still a day earlier in Hawaii! He flies and delivers gifts around the clock, working more than twenty-four hours—but he's always there before the kids get up on Christmas morning.

One thing that enables Santa to make his 'round-the-world trip so quickly is that he almost never touches ground. By going from rooftop to rooftop, he cuts out a good part of his descent with each stop.

After his Christmas trip, Santa needs days of recuperation. During that period, the elves are even nicer than usual.

Mrs. Santa has a special cup of hot chocolate all ready and waiting when Santa arrives back home.

After his long, long ride, he finally arrives home, dead tired. He's gone for all those hours without sleep—and all he had to eat during the whole time was some food Mrs. Santa packed and the cookies and milk along the way. (And, of course, the reindeer are just as tired and hungry.) By now Santa is too exhausted even to walk, so the elves take him out of the sleigh and carry him in to his bed. Around the world children are joyously opening their gifts—but Santa is snoring away up at the North Pole! Another happy, successful, totally fatiguing Christmas!

46

How the Elves First Met Santa

Limlim the Hunter dwelt with his people in the farthest reaches of the Canadian forest. Every day he went forth to find food for all the others. They ate well because of Limlim's skill, enjoying the juiciest meat, the plumpest berries, the tastiest spring water.

The elves were happy, and they were safe.

Then one day a fire raged through their forest. The elves fled before it—and when they returned a charred blackness was all that remained.

Limlim sat down on a blackened stump and wept. The elves' home was gone. Their animal friends were all dead. Nothing remained but sorrow.

But when Limlim finally raised his weeping, downcast eyes, he saw that the others had little sorrow. His wife came close and tugged his beard impishly. "Life was meant to be merry," she cried. "Find us meat, Limlim, and we'll all rejoice that at least we can eat!"

Limlim stood steadfastly before them and made a vow, tweaking his ears in emphasis, as is the elvish custom: "I will find meat for my people. I will not return unsuccessful."

The people began to rebuild their homes, and Limlim set off alone through what remained of the forest. Where before he had seen lush greenness all around, now there was only death and destruction from the fire. Where before there had been rabbits and squirrels and deer all around, now Limlim could find only burnt carcasses.

He hunted through the day—and saw no game. That night he went to bed hungry, worried about his people, sick at the devastation he saw in every direction.

The next day he arose and continued his search, and the next—and the next. Each day he grew weaker and weaker. He began to despair of ever finding anything for his people. He began to fear that even if he did find food, he would arrive back too late.

Then he saw the tracks. An enormous snow deer! Limlim had never seen such huge tracks before. He knelt close to the ground and thrust his nose right up to one of the tracks. It was fresh! The deer had passed only moments before!

Knowing that game was near gave Limlim new strength. He knew that he was right on the edge of the frozen snow country, but he paid that no heed. He quickly followed the deer out onto the snow and began to track it across the rolling hills that led ever farther north.

For two days Limlim followed the deer. It was always just beyond him, always just over the next rise.

Finally dusk came on that second day and Limlim knew he could go no farther. He went for more than a mile on his hands and knees, crawling painfully over the hard, crusted snow. The bitter chill bit through his clothes, making him shiver violently, and the snow cut his hands.

"I'll die in this frozen wasteland," he cried hoarsely, and then his strength left him and he fell on his face into the snow.

That night a fierce storm arose. Wind blew harshly across Limlim's still body. Snow began to drift onto his near-frozen hands and face, covering them. The snow felt strangely warm to Limlim. "Wonderful, wonderful," he muttered, and he slipped into a dream.

He saw himself sitting by a comfortable hearth, warming his hands at the hot fire. Right beside him was a drink of hot brew someone had prepared for him. On his feet were thick and heavy skins, expertly wrapped.

"Ah," he smiled to himself. "May I ever sit warmly by this fire, drinking hot brew. If this is heaven, it's even better than I'd hoped! All I lack is some steaming meat, my family, and a few friends."

The thought of his family and friends stopped the dream. Limlim woke up, feeling stiff and numb. He slowly opened his eyes, groggy, and looked around him. The wind had stopped and the moon shone above, shining clear and bright across the new-fallen snow. And there, far on the horizon, was *someone else!*

Limlim tried to rise, tried to raise his hand to hail the man, tried to shout for help. But the effort was too great. All he could do was get his frozen fingers to twitch. All he could do was croak out a sound. Utterly weak and nearly dead, Limlim fell back into the snow.

The next thing he knew he was riding on a burly back through the deep snow. Wrapped around him was the man's own coat. His stomach gnawed with hunger—but his coldness was gone. Instead he felt a marvelous warmth radiating from the man who had saved him from death.

"My friends, my friends," Limlim suddenly whispered, tears welling in his cold eyes. He realized that the man had saved him, but that his friends were probably near death themselves.

The man heard his whisper. "Your friends are safe," the man said in a deep, rich voice. "I have sent help."

Nothing more was said. Limlim let himself go limp on the man's back. After many hours they entered a broad valley with buildings. The valley radiated warmth in the same way the man did. In the center of the valley stood a pole. Limlim had heard of it in talks over the campfire at night: the North Pole.

And then he knew. The man was Santa Claus.

"I thought you were only a story!" Limlim said, his voice full of amazement.

"A story!" Santa bellowed. "Only a story! You'd better be thankful this man who is only a story was around to save your life!" And then he laughed so hard Limlim was afraid he would fall off.

Santa and Mrs. Claus nursed Limlim back to health, first feeding him some warm broth and gradually working up to specially aged meat. It was three weeks before he felt he could travel again.

But he didn't want to leave. Santa had found a new forest for his people, and Limlim knew they could find a new Hunter.

"I want to stay with you forever, Santa," Limlim said. "I pledge my life to your service. I pledge the service of my family. We will be with you as long as the world is. Such is the only way an elf can repay a debt of life. You gave me my life when I was frozen in the snow, and now I give you my life."

And so it was that the elves began to serve Santa. Limlim was the first. He lived very long, even for an elf, until he was 452. But then he grew old and died. After him, his sons served; and then their sons. They find great joy in serving Santa Claus. And they love to repeat the story of how Santa saved Limlim by carrying him on his back. No story is more often told among Santa's elves.

They are there—Limlim's great family of elves—serving Santa to this very day.

Waking Up the Elves

After the frantic Christmas days, the elves go to bed to hibernate in a long winter's nap—for five months. They sleep right through all the excitement of the spring's activities, including the reindeer's spring mating (with all its racket) and the noisy spring cleaning in the neighboring hall. They also sleep right through the noise of Santa's daily breakfast joke (which they've probably already heard anyway) with his uproarious laughter and Mrs. Claus's off-key singing in the shower.

Sometime after midnight on New Year's Eve they start heading for their cots; by noon every one of them is tucked in. January passes uneventfully. In February a couple of the elves start to snore and snort. In March one or two of the light sleepers get up to go to the bathroom (some years).

Then on the first of June, promptly at 8 a.m., Santa takes a break from his gardening to wake up the first elf. Gald usually has the distinction of being the first up, being an early riser. A time or two, however, Santa has been unsuccessful with Gald—then he tries Romo as a back-up. Romo would just as soon forego the privilege.

Waking up an elf is almost a lost art, except around the North Pole. Santa starts with an extra-long quill from the wing of a pure-white snow goose. He lightly tickles under the elf's nose, very gently. After several minutes of no response the elf will suddenly, totally without warning, sneeze out with such a noise that it awakens him. (Santa is always careful to stand to the side when he tickles.)

If the sneeze is unsuccessful, Santa will try again.

But that's only the first step. After the elf's eyes open a crack, Santa seizes his opportunity in his right hand. He grasps the elf's bulbous nose firmly and massages it until the elf is alert and growling. Then he props the elf against the back of the bed while he takes a day or two to more completely come to his senses.

It's Gald's job to awaken the others. As you might imagine, it's an odious and thankless task. But then he's also the first one to breakfast. Every job has its high points.

Watch out for a newly awakened elf. He can't see clearly, and his thinking is even more muddled than his sight. If you approach him too quickly, he may mistake you for live mutton. *Avoid sudden moves.*

Mrs. Claus has a freshly laundered towel waiting on each elf's trunk, as well as a fresh toothbrush. Unless she's sick, which *has* happened. The first time the elves complained mightily, but nothing was to be done. "We'll make the best of a bad thing, boys," Gald shouted, clapping them on the backs. Old Stout snarled back at him, but soon enough they were all on their way to the bathroom, stumbling and bleary-eyed. After drinking a gallon or two of water each they felt a little better about the whole thing.

But you can be sure Stout mentioned it in Mrs. Claus's hearing over the breakfast table.

An elf, just awakened. Note the eyes: they mean murder until the elf is really awake.

Tooth brushing comes first. Not even an elf wants to walk around reeking bad breath. Teeth usually have a fine green mold on them after a five months' sleep. This is true even in humans. One brush is usually adequate to the task, though toothpaste must be applied liberally.

The toothbrush must be held very firmly to make the brushing effective. Note how the little finger is outstretched. This is a toothbrush-holding technique peculiar to the elves of the North Pole. The elf closes his eyes while he brushes, lest the green film from his teeth flip into them.

The Green Grunge

When the elf brushes his teeth after his long hibernation, a green grunge flips off into the sink. Earlier observations suggested that the grunge was simply bacterial mold.

An enlarged view of the green grunge, magnified 16 million times. At this power of magnification, the gold and copper are easily seen, as are other trace metals.

But closer scrutiny showed that it was actually a thin layer of copper and gold, which was a by-product of the elf's peculiar metabolism.

Elves have no use for such metals. Their medium of exchange is traditionally "favors," and "word of honor." The idea of precious metals is meaningless to them.

Millennia ago the elves were approached by a renowned scientist from Atlantis, The Honorable Hemit Dentist. Dentist had learned of the metals on their teeth and struck up a deal where he paid them to clean it off. He then sold the copper and gold grunge to metals collectors; his profits were used to fund further research.

The Honorable Hemit Dentist never worked on other than elvish teeth. His work, however, soon became a tradition among civilized worlds, and rich people began to have their barbers clean their teeth in the effort to find gold. People who had no gold in their teeth hired the barber to put some in. Some barbers took up the trade full time. They called themselves . . . *dentists.*

The Honorable Hemit Dentist, shown with some of the tools of his trade.

Sources:
—Traditions recounted among the Zuul tribes of Upper Siberia.

—Parchment fragments ascribed to Lulius Orpius, a monk of the third-century order of the Beloved Brotherhood.
—Archives of the American Dental Association.

Baths are taken in an assembly line. First one bathed has to tote water for the next in line. (Not Gald; he's done his job.) From the clean water bucket onto the head, soap all around. From the sudsy water into a clean tub. Rinse. Hop out nimbly, dancing around in the chill. No women allowed, of course. Dry vigorously. The whole bathing process goes quite quickly. It takes only about three hours each.

Unless you fall asleep in the rinsing tub, which old Zeeker does every single year.

Here we see the gamut of clean water (being poured over the head) to dirty water (surrounding the nude elf in the tub). The elf with the bucket wrinkles his nose to resist the smell of soggy elf, which can be very offensive. Note how the elf holds the scrub brush with his little finger outstretched. This technique is peculiar to the elves of the North Pole.

Each elf takes about forty-five gallons of water and one pound of special cleansing soap to get clean. Another twenty gallons of water are used for rinsing. Then the elf need bathe no oftener than once every nine days.

Soap recipe: Mix together one pound of denatured lye, six pounds of strained polar bear tallow, and a quart of cold water. Heat over a low flame, about 120 degrees. Stir until thoroughly mixed, Pour in a dab of Canadian pine oil to make it smell good. Remove from the flame, pour into sheets, and let cure for at least two weeks.

53

The fingernails and toenails of an elf don't grow much faster than those of a human—but when the growth is compounded, uncut, for many months on end, the result is very noticeable.

Clipped toenails are not discarded but are stored in an airtight jar. Once the jar is filled, the nails are shipped to Nice, France, where a factory grinds them up and processes them into an ointment. The ointment is particularly useful on the sores reindeer get from the straps attached to the sleigh.

Haircutting. It's no easy task on an elf. First, because his hair is as thick and heavy as a mangy Saint Bernard's. Second, because it's grown so scraggly over the five-month sleep. And third, because the elf won't sit still—haircuts tickle excruciatingly!

Upper cheeks are shaved, hair on ears is cut (with very sharp scissors), hair on the bulb of the nose is cut (except for the elves who are too old-fashioned to have it done), finger and toenails are clipped. Very carefully. The nails are like spears, and more than one elf has suffered a serious wound for want of taking care.

Elves take turns at being barber—though some definitely do a better job at it than others. The barber elf wears a cap against the cold air in the room. Singing is a favorite activity to while away the long process of cutting an elf's coarse hair. Typical tune: "Joggy, Joggy, Jug-a-way."

Elf Hair

Elf hair is tough and resilient. Like everything else elvish, clipped hair has a secondary use: it is woven together to make elvish clothing. Of course the elves also wear cotton and wool, but those aren't nearly as comfortable or as durable as elf hair. Because elf hair is in rare supply, some articles of clothing take years to make.

Elf hair

A finished tunic for a young elf.

54

Breaking into the routine somewhere is bathroom time. One visit of thirty or forty minutes usually does it, but it seems like some of the older elves are in there *constantly*. But after five months, who can blame them?

It's nearly a day before the elves are presentable enough to go to breakfast. It's a real hardship—for two-and-a-half months they've been dreaming of food. Two months of sleep is no problem for an elf's stomach. He hardly even notices it. Much. But after two-and-a-half months, he starts to wriggle a little in his sleep. Dreams start to creep into his head. His ears twitch a little (though he doesn't know it), and he starts to smack his lips. Over and over. Smack. Smack. Smack.

They get up a regular smacking chorus. Smacking and dreaming of food. Mounds and piles and mountains and hills and valleys and rivers and snowbanks and icebergs and warehouses of *food*. Mutton and ale, potatoes and carrots, beef and more beef and bacon and mutton.

Finally: breakfast. Gald has eaten his fill; he sits there on his stool grinning foolishly and belching while he watches the others uncouthly gulp down helping after helping. On the first serving there is usually a little strategy, each elf trying to outmaneuver the other for a little more food, gotten to a little sooner.

But there is plenty for all. They're able to eat as long as they want, and still the food keeps coming. The meal goes on for eighteen hours, sometimes twenty.

When the elves are finally full, they stumble fatly back to their beds. Naptime for a day. Naptime to dream of not being so fatly full. Naptime to dream of being skinny, slender, thin, comfortable in the joyous feeling of hungrily sitting down, empty, to a full table.

The feeling quickly goes away, though, and sleep comes on fully. One last nap before the work starts.

At this point in the day the elf's eyes are beginning to get some humor (and life) into them. His head is scrubbed; his beard is clipped; his fingernails are cut. He almost looks *normal*! And now he's ready to get into some two-fisted eating action. The menu includes several servings of pancakes each, specially prepared elf mash, and goat's milk, freshly obtained from the nanny.

Interesting Elvish Words

The language of the elves is ancient and highly developed. Some branches of elves were speaking complex sentences long before Chinese and Hebrew were even thought of!

It's interesting to see how thoroughly the elves have contributed to modern-day English. The following words (which are only a very small sampling of the many I could cite) will demonstrate:

Okey-dokey. Used by the elves when everything is "just okay." (Such words as this have also been influential in the development of such languages as Korean.)

Alrighty-dighty. Has a similar meaning to *okey-dokey*, but more intensive.

Blabbermouth. An English corruption of "blubbermouth," referring to a person with fat lips.

Doo-hinkey. An inexpensive item with an unknown proper name.

Dingledorf. (1) The sound made by reindeer bells during a heavy snowfall. (2) A muffling. Often used in English to refer to a silly or stupid person, whose wits are "muffled."

Bugaboo. A small, scary insect. (People in America and Europe often discount the existence of the bugaboo, being unaware that it's invisible except during molting season.)

Hubba-hubba. What an elf says when he's especially excited.

Elvish Presley. Used to indicate a small species of singing elves who have double-jointed hips.

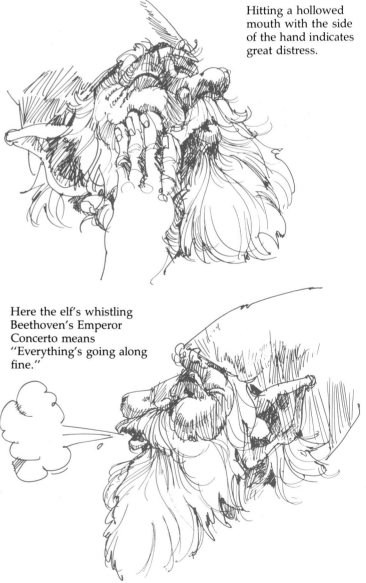

Hitting a hollowed mouth with the side of the hand indicates great distress.

Here the elf's whistling Beethoven's Emperor Concerto means "Everything's going along fine."

Sources:
—Webster's Old Collegiate Dictionary, 1st ed., 1823, special article entitled "Unusual Language Correlatives," pp. 1327-39.
—Limlim III, *A Guide to Elvish Rhetorial Rhetoric,* manuscript fragments, North Pole Archives.

Upper Mucky. (1) A river in Nigeria, noted for its dirtiness. The Lower Mucky is a tributary. (2) The wig of a rich person that's gone too long without a shampoo.

Supercalifragilisticexpialidocious. Something that's exceptionally neat. (Popularized by Walter Elias Disney in the latter part of the twentieth century.)

Goon. (1) A bully elf. (2) A long dress worn by a female elf for formal occasions, often referred to as an "evening goon."

Hoity-Toity. (1) A polite way of saying, "I gotta go to the bathroom!" (2) A person who thinks she's hot stuff.

Mukluk. A boot used for walking across mucky ground. As the boot slurps up out of the muck it makes a peculiar sound: "Luk . . . luk . . . luk. . . ."

Nerd. (1)The unhatched egg of a Dodo bird. (2) Extended in meaning by some to refer to the unhatched brain of a "nerdish" human.

Groovy. A long, unending rut.

Peachy Keen. Exact meaning is unknown, as is etymology—yet elves use the expression whenever they see something they like.

Super-Duper. The largest and most impressive Dupers known to elves. (Sometimes spelled Sooper-Dooper by the unschooled.)

Modern Elvish

Nowadays elves and humans have very little contact. But many millennia ago, certain groups of humans and certain species of elves interacted freely. And one group of people, the Welsh, loved and revered the elves so greatly that they eventually adopted their language.

800In essence, then, modern Welsh and modern Elvish are the same (except for the normal deviations that occur in any language). In fact, on the rare occasion when an elf appears to a Welshman, they are able to communicate with one another clearly. The Welsh are the only humans on earth who are able to use and understand the Elvish language.

The Welsh adoption of Elvish is fortunate for us, since it enables us to get a better understanding of the elves' language than we otherwise would be able to.

Here are a few English words and their Elvish equivalents:

porridge—uwd (uwd is one of the elves' least
favorite foods)
gherkin—math o gucumer (one of the elves'
most favorite foods)
Christmas—Nadolig
reindeer—carw Llychlyn
joy—llawenydd
jingle—gwneud swn felcloch
sleigh—car illusg

And here's how the elves count from 1 to 20. Note the similarities between their system and the English system. And note the inner logic of their language:

1—un	8—wyth	15—pymtheg
2—dau	9—naw	16—un ar bymtheg
3—tri	10—deg	17—dau ar bymtheg
4—pedwar	11—un ar ddeg	18—deunaw
5—pump	12—deuddeg	19—pedwar ar bymtheg
6—chwech	13—tri ar ddeg	20—ugain
7—saith	14—pedwar ar ddeg	

Since elves find human languages so difficult, Santa has had to learn Elvish in order to communicate with his helpers.

Three Things You Should Know About Elves

There are three things everyone should know about elves. In fact, if you knew nothing else about elves, you should at least know these three things.

1

Every elf wishes he were a cowboy. In fact, some experts have speculated that all cowboys *are* elves, in disguise!

Cowboys must be tall and *macho*. And elves are neither. So the elves invented the cowboy boot (see Item 2, below). And to be more macho, some elves speak in a deep voice and say such things as: "Yup!" "Y'hear?" "Say, hey, there, dude!" and "Wanna step outside?"

2

Elves wear lifters. Ever since the cave-elf first discovered the magic of fire, elves have been self-conscious about their height. They're unable to reach things they need to, and when they dance with humans they find themselves staring right into their navels. Or knees. To help correct these problems, elves now wear lifters. But it's almost impossible to see the lifters an elf is wearing, they've been so subtly designed.

3

Elves sing a song that has mystical overtones. The song, called "Joggy, Joggy, Jug-a-way," has secret meaning to the elves—though they'll tell no outsider what that meaning is. I include a verse of the song below, in the hopes that you may be able to decipher its meaning. (Should you be successful, please write me and let me know what you've discovered.)

Joggy, Joggy, Jug-a-way

oh jog-gy jog-gy jug-a-way. We work and work no time for play. For we are hap-py lit-tle elves and we make toys for San-ta's shelves. Oh myme-bo myme-bo Care-a-lay, oh og-gle dog-gle dare-a-day. We'll sing until the world is gray, We'll touch your dreams but will not stay.

The Elves' Incredible Strength

One of the best examples of body strength in the world is the ant. An ant can lift up to 50 times its body weight.

That means that if a 200-pound man could lift the same proportion as an ant, he'd be able to lift *five tons*—or 3 elephants!

But compared to an elf, the strength of an ant is *nothing*. **Elves can lift 150 times their body weight!** That incredible power doesn't come just from arm or leg muscles. Every part of the body works together to lift loads that would stagger even a dump truck.

For example, the bones in an elf's arm can withstand pressures that would burst the bones of any other creature on earth.

Elvish intestines can process enormous amounts of food, giving the elf much-needed energy.

Muscles in an elf's leg, when tensed, become so hard that rocks can be broken against them.

The elf's amazingly broad foot, when squeezed into his narrow slippers, gives him the kind of balance high-wire artists work years to attain.

The elf's brain is quite large in proportion to his body, which enables him to psych himself up for the difficult task of lifting more than two tons of assorted items. (The brain is nearly as large in raw measurement as that of the dolphin, even though the dolphin is much larger overall.)

The 200-pound man I referred to earlier would be able to lift *fifteen* tons—or 9 elephants—if he had the power of an elf.

An ant is incredibly strong for its size—but the elf is even stronger!

It's amazing to think that an elf could lift a family of elephants. But it's even more amazing to consider the bulk he has to carry out to the sleigh on the night before Christmas. And then he goes back and gets another load just as big!

Once an elf gets up to his mature strength, his only challenge is learning to balance all that stuff! To help young elves master the technique, more experienced elves put them through several years of training, as they gradually develop the ability to handle the bulkiness of the weight they're capable of carrying.

They first learn how to carry books. Once they've mastered that, the instructor elves have them learn the technique of bikes and trikes, which can be quite complicated when you're dealing with several dozen of them. Finally they get the whole thing down, and they're able to carry their share in the laborious process of loading Santa's bag full enough of toys for all the good children in the world.

Elvish strength comes in handy in other ways, too, as when reindeer won't cooperate and step into the harness: the elf can just *lift* them in!

A Typical Elf Load:

100 pounds of dolls	100 pounds of board games
100 pounds of doll clothes	50 pounds of musical instruments
200 pounds of trains and trucks	250 pounds of garage sets
50 pounds of B-B guns	250 pounds of farm sets
400 pounds of bikes and trikes	100 pounds of kids' jewelry
200 pounds of outdoor games	200 pounds of perfumes and other toiletries
400 pounds of clothes	
100 pounds of stuffed toys	500 pounds of toy stoves, refrigerators, cabinets, cookware, etc.
150 pounds of books	
250 pounds of baby toys	800-some-odd pounds of assorted other items
150 pounds of electronic games	
150 pounds of building toys	

Santa can lift everything an elf lifts—plus the elf!

Zeeker's Favorite Story

Here's a true story told by Zeeker the elf—the greatest storyteller in the world!

Long, long ago there lived a little creature called the Loud-Mouth Twit, and he was mean as mean can be! The twit liked to stand on your shoulder and whisper in your ear, giving you bad ideas. He'd make you crabby and moody, and you wouldn't even notice he was there. That's the kind of a fellow this nasty twit was!

The Trouble with Presents. We put up with that Loud-Mouth Twit for a long time. But when he started causing trouble with our presents, we figured we had to do something.

Back then, people liked to give presents to other people, just like they do now. And back then, the giver liked to surprise the receiver, just like now. That was half the fun.

So whenever an elf would make a present, he'd hide it until gift-giving day came around. Then, on the gift-day, the elf would pull out that gift and give it to his friend. "Oh, thank you, thank you; I had no idea; it's just what I wanted; oh, thanks so much!" the receiver would say. And everyone would be happy.

Twits don't like people to be happy. It makes them mad. It shrivels up their faces and makes their claws come out. Oh, twits are mean that way!

And the Loud-Mouth Twit was the worst one of all. "It's the surprise they like best," he muttered to himself. "I can't stop this stupid gift-giving, but I *can* ruin the surprise!"

And that's what he set out to do. Whenever an elf would hide a gift, the twit would find it. And then, like the Loud-Mouth Twit he was, he'd jump on the shoulder of the other elf and whisper in his ear: "Hey, old Amt is getting you a new chair for gift-day! How about that! It's made of mahogany and the seat is covered with red velvet, and he's planning to surprise you. Heh-heh-heh!"

The twit's tail is as mean and nasty as the twit himself. In technical terminology, it's called a *tattletail*, though some experts call it the *telltail*.

61

Then the surprise was all ruined, and half the fun was gone.

That made the Loud-Mouth Twit very happy. "They hate it!" he chuckled gleefully. "Their gift-day isn't any fun any longer!"

Well, elves aren't dumb. They knew that sneaky twit was whispering in their ears! The solution was to hide their gifts a lot better.

So they tried hiding presents under the floor of the Elf Hall. They hid them under the step. In the drainpipes. Under the ceiling. On top of the roof. Out in the bushes. Under the outhouse seat. Under their pillows. Wherever they could think of that the twit wouldn't find them.

But that didn't stop the Loud-Mouth Twit! Twits have very sharp eyes and a keen sense of smell. The Loud-Mouth Twit was able to find every gift they hid—and then he went running to the recipient. "Oh noble Willo!" he'd sing in the elf's ear. "Erdi is getting you something wonderful for gift-day! A yellow-green blanket to go on your bed, with striped fringes of amber and gold. Made out of Erdi's own hair, that he's been saving all these years. Isn't this a wonderful surprise! Oh, won't you be so surprised?"

Then, when Erdi gave the precious blanket to Willo, instead of being happy and surprised, Willo only said, "Oh, yes, I knew you were going to give this to me. Oh, well, okay."

Things finally got so bad that the elves called an Elf Council.

"We've got to stop this Loud-Mouth Twit," the leader said. "He's ruining *everything*."

They discussed the problem all day and through the night. And then, finally, one of the youngest elves had an idea. "Why don't we cover our presents, so the twit can't see inside?"

"And what would we cover them with, young one?" the leader asked sternly.

"Oh, I don't know," the young elf answered. "How about paper?"

As soon as the elf said it, all the others knew that was their answer. They'd cover the gifts with paper!

The next day all the elves got busy making new gifts, for a special gift-day. One by one they completed their projects—and then wrapped the presents in paper. They tried to find colorful, pretty, bright paper, to make the gift look nicer, and some even wrapped the package in a bow. Then they put all the presents in a stack by the window.

When the twit came along, he sneered at the elves. "Hah!" he said. "Presents! I'm going to take a little peek." And he sneaked up to the pile and tried to look. But twits are weak, and the paper was strong. He tried package after package—and he couldn't see inside even one of them.

"Oh, woe! Oh, misery!" he shouted. "The elves are going to be surprised and have half their fun!" In his frustration and despair he raced from the Elf Hall—and he's never been seen again.

Ever since then the elves have had great fun surprising each other on gift-day. They say, "Oh, thank you, thank you! I had no idea! It was just what I wanted!" And they've found that wrapping packages makes gifts *twice* as fun as they were before!

Note: When Zeeker finished his story, he yawned and stretched, and then said slyly, "Oh, by the way. I didn't tell you who that smart young elf was, the one who thought of the idea of wrapping paper. Well, his name starts with a Z, if you know what I mean!

How Santa Makes Toys

It's a pretty well-known fact that no one can make toys like Santa Claus and his elves. There are companies around the world that make toys, and their toys are usually pretty good, but they're *nothing* like the toys that Santa makes.

There are several ways to tell a Santa-made toy:

1. No ebony or magnesium parts. (Santa is allergic to both.)

2. Extra-fine craftsmanship.

3. Innovative designs.

Santa's toys are *not* available in stores—though toy companies frequently copy his designs. Santa doesn't merchandise the things he makes, but saves them all for gifts. (If he tried to supply the world with all its toys, he'd never get done!)

Santa has been in the toy-making business for so long that he's developed production techniques that are unrivaled anywhere in the world. Shortly after World War II, the Japanese sent a representative to Santa to learn his production secrets. Santa told him just one word: "Kimche-ku"—and by applying that secret the Japanese have since become one of the greatest industrial nations in the world.

On the following page are shown the production steps of a typical toy. Santa's design and the elves'

know-how combine to make the system work. But just as important is the machinery Santa has developed. His doll machine, for instance, can produce doll bodies, doll hair, doll eyes, and doll clothes with very little supervision. And the train machine, shown on the next page, can make up to 30 trains a minute (or one every two seconds) when it's at the peak of production.

One of Santa's most important toy-making machines, the doll-hair fastener-on.

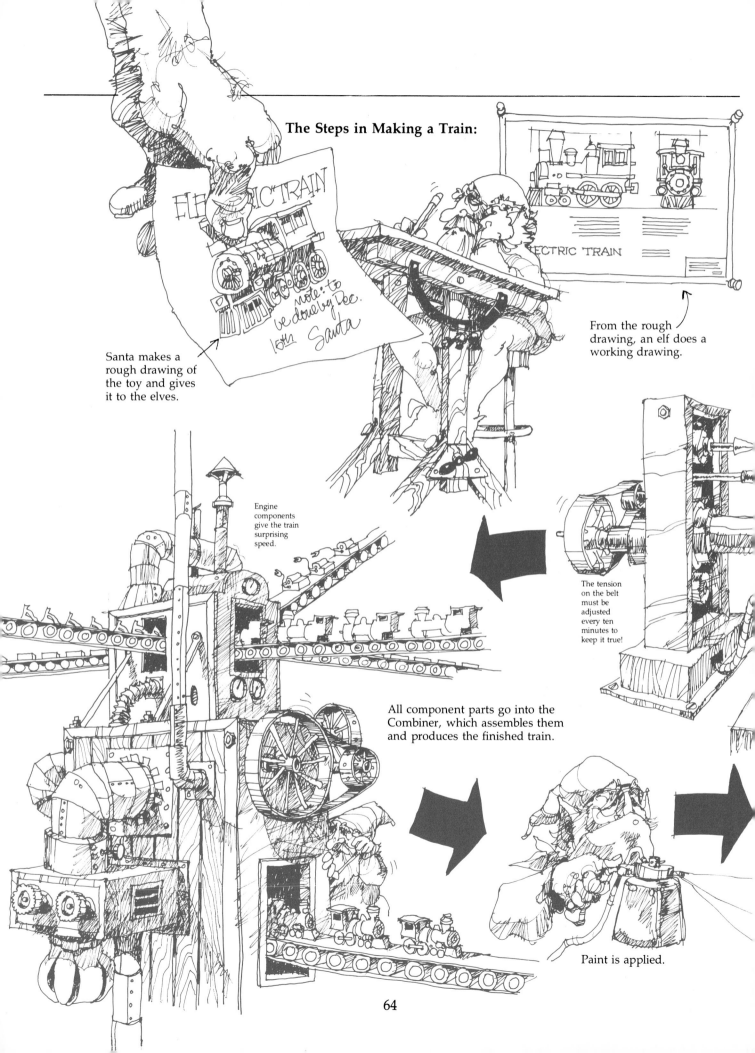

The Steps in Making a Train:

Santa makes a rough drawing of the toy and gives it to the elves.

note: to be done by Dec. 15th Santa

From the rough drawing, an elf does a working drawing.

Engine components give the train surprising speed.

The tension on the belt must be adjusted every ten minutes to keep it true!

All component parts go into the Combiner, which assembles them and produces the finished train.

Paint is applied.

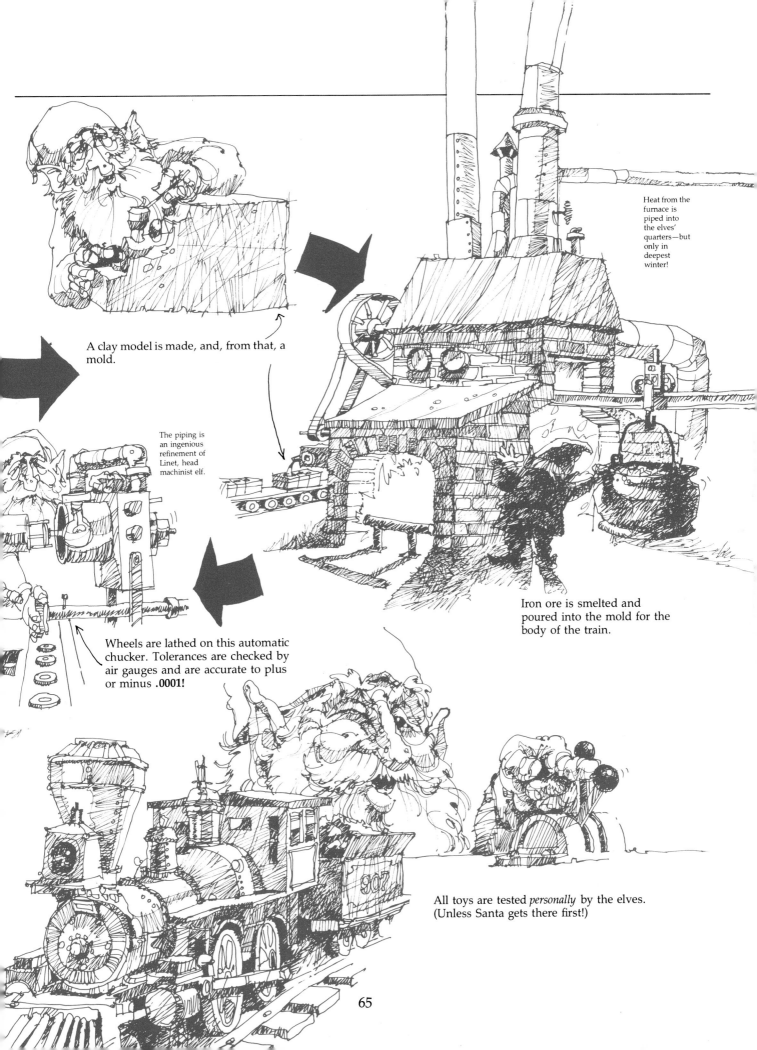

A clay model is made, and, from that, a mold.

Heat from the furnace is piped into the elves' quarters—but only in deepest winter!

The piping is an ingenious refinement of Linet, head machinist elf.

Iron ore is smelted and poured into the mold for the body of the train.

Wheels are lathed on this automatic chucker. Tolerances are checked by air gauges and are accurate to plus or minus **.0001!**

All toys are tested *personally* by the elves. (Unless Santa gets there first!)

The Elves' Surprise Parties

If there's one thing that distinguishes an elf, it's this: elves *love* to throw parties. It doesn't matter what day it is. It doesn't matter whether it's snow or shine outside. If they're awake, you can bet they're probably planning a party.

One of their favorite surprise parties is for Santa's birthday. No one knows for sure when Santa was born (not even Santa), so no one can say for sure when his birthday should be celebrated. The elves' solution: celebrate it on lots of days! That way, chances are, they'll hit the real day. And in the meantime they get to have parties!

The elves have had so many great parties it's impossible even to mention all of them. But here are two that were especially good:

The Sleigh Surprise Party. One Christmas the elves decided to have a surprise party on Christmas Eve. That would mean they'd have to delay their hibernation by a day or so, but for a party it would be worth it. When the sleigh was just about all loaded, the elves wrapped each other up in gift boxes, and put the boxes into Santa's bag. Finally everyone was loaded up but Raful. He found Santa, yawned real big, and said, "We've got the sleigh loaded up, and everyone's gone to bed. We just couldn't wait. We'll see you in late spring."

Santa's pre-Christmas nap was interrupted at 2 a.m. of the second night with an elves' surprise shish-kabob party.

When the elves prepare for a party, they go all out. Their gifts are the finest that can be found anywhere.

When the elves threw a party in the outhouse, Santa really *was* surprised!

Then Raful yawned again, and stretched wide, making a moaning sound. "It's sure been a hard season!" he exclaimed. And he went off in the direction of the elf hall.

But when Santa wasn't looking, Raful jumped into the bag on the sleigh. Everyone was ready.

Poor unsuspecting Santa went out and climbed on his sleigh. "On Dasher! On Dancer!" he called. The reindeer lifted up and flew into the sky. The night was dark and cold. Santa reached under the sleigh seat for his hot chocolate. It wasn't there. "Those blasted elves," Santa muttered. "Going to bed before their job is done!"

Just then his bag flew open. Packages began to burst, and out popped elf after elf. "Surprise!" they called. "Surprise!" Then they sang "Happy Birthday," up there in the sky traveling faster than anything; and then they brought out the cake and the, yep, the hot chocolate!

The Outhouse Surprise Party. It wasn't too long ago that Santa didn't have indoor plumbing. Everyone had to use the outdoor john—

Santa and Mrs. Santa *thought* they were going to have a few minutes alone. . . .

which isn't too exciting in cold weather. One day the elves were thinking of how uncomfortable the old outhouse really was—and they decided to brighten up Santa's day the next time he had to use it. So they got a party ready. Santa trudged out across the snow to the quarter moon. Opened the door. Shut. The elves waited. Held their breath. Counted to twenty. Then they opened the door. "Surprise!"

Santa Puts His Foot Down. Finally the elves got so busy throwing parties that they weren't doing their work. And Santa couldn't get any done either. So he made a rule: only one birthday surprise party per year.

At first the elves were pretty upset. They could

celebrate other things, of course, but it just wasn't the same as Santa's birthday. Then they decided to really go all out on their next surprise party. They planned and planned. Finally it was ready.

One day Santa went into his bathroom to take his bath. He closed and locked the door. He poured in the hot, steaming water. He got undressed. He climbed into the tub. Then, suddenly, the elves popped out of the towel closets. They jumped out from under the tub. And they splashed right into the tub with Santa! "Surprise!"

It was their finest moment!

Santa thought he had the parties under control—until the elves hopped into the tub with him!

Note: The elves will throw a party at a drop of a hat. Because of this, Santa has proclaimed a city ordinance that it's illegal for *anyone* to drop his hat!

69

Twelve
Magic Words

Far back in the almost forgotten lore of the elves is an exhaustive store of magic—in olden times the elves were able to do all sorts of wondrous things with their magic.

Unfortunately, most of that has been lost. All that has come to the elves over the years is twelve magic words, instead of the thousands they used to have. Those twelve can be very powerful. Yet they don't solve all the elves' problems. Each word becomes effective only when it's spoken after first drinking the FRUMP potion—and the potion is ever in short supply.

Santa uses the Twelfth Word to rise up chimneys.

The Twelve Magic Words:

One: Dinky Doiley. Used by an elf to make himself invisible. The difficulty is that the word for making oneself visible again has been lost.

Two: KalamazamKalamazoo! Spoken to make an object disappear. Doesn't work for anything larger than a whale. (A group of elves once used this on a polar bear. He disappeared—and they didn't see a thing when he chewed them up.)

Three: Hogey Bogey. Works to clean a room within seconds. The magic may not put things where you want them, however. Thim once used this and found all his dirty clothes stuffed down the toilet.

Four: Peepeepoopoo. Magically transforms your enemy into the animal you're thinking of at the time. Be careful not to think of a vicious animal—turkeys and squirrels are good choices.

Five: Yup-Yup. Effective when you want a plant to grow fast. Elvish records show that Jack didn't really have magic beans; he just knew how to use Yup-Yup magic.

Six: Bully Bully! Turns raw materials into the toy of your choice. Must be spoken very loudly and with great force. (Hans Leeflang of Holland tried this one once—and he was thinking of every toy he'd ever wanted. He was trapped under the resulting toys for three days before they could dig him out. Teddy Roosevelt used a variation of this magic spell to become president of the United States.)

Seven: Piggy Pog. Cures just about any imaginable illness. Does not work for cut fingers or for colds, however.

Eight: Higgledy Piggledy Poo. Good for changing the weather. Can make it go from snow to rain within seconds, or from cloudiness to clear skies. *Beware:* When you give yourself nice weather, you're stealing it from someone else, and giving them your clouds.

Nine: Bunko Bucky Bah-Bah. Make someone shut up. When the noise gets to an elf, if he has some potion handy, he says the magic words and the other person is unable to speak for 55 minutes.

Ten: Joe Betchum. Said to bring something to mind. Works to help the elf remember things he's forgotten, as well as things he never knew before.

Eleven: Rumplestiltskin. Pronounced to bring a shiny star down into your hand.

Twelve: Huppy Huppy Ho-Ho-Ho! Must be said with a broad smile, and with the finger on the side of the nose. Works to make an elf go up into the air. The elves taught this spell to Santa to enable him to go up chimneys.

The FRUMP Potion

None of this magic does any good unless the elf first swallows at least a teaspoon of the FRUMP Potion. Some of the ingredients of the potion are hard to come by, and a batch won't last without spoiling for more than three weeks. To make the potion, gather the following ingredients and boil them over a medium hot flame.

F: Fine Hair of a Frozen Flea, chopped into tiny pieces.
R: Righteous Indignation of a Mad Mayfly (at least 10.52 grams).
U: Urn with umbones of a Red Wooger (at least 23 gallons).
M: Music from the Stars, gathered during the Full Moon.
P: Purple Hair from Witch Hazel (2 strands).

Let the potion cool for at least one hour before ingesting.

Games Elves Play

Elves are great game players. They can mess around with a single game for hours on end and never get tired. And they're always good sports. An elf never worries about losing or looking foolish in a game. All he cares about is the fun he's having while he plays.

Leapfrog. One of their favorite games is leapfrog. The first step in this game is finding the frogs. In fact, that's half the fun. Once each elf has found—and caught—a large frog, they're ready to play. When the frogs are caught, they're already lined up in a row. Then, with a running start, the elves leap over one after another.

The frogs don't have to do much but wait patiently. When the game is over, the elves let them go until next time.

Leapfrog can be great fun if the frogs are large enough.

The frogs are caught when they eat a Winkiti fly that's been attached to a stake. The frog refuses to let go of the fly and thus is stuck until the elves let him go.

Sources:
—Ann Phibian, *Memoirs*, Winnebago: Happy Day Publishing, 1980, pp. 15-19.
—Amos Quito, *Fun with Frogs*, London: Big Bug Books, 1959, pp. 100-123.

Formation Flying. This game was devised by Limlim as he was training the first reindeer. It works only when the reindeer are in a mood to play. Each elf trains a group of deer for the great competition. Then, on the assigned day, the reindeer put on a dazzling display of formation flying. The prize to the winning elf: No more cleaning out stables for the rest of the year!

This particular formation was the winner the year I watched. The winning elf was a young upstart named Ii.

Mush Face. This is a game that has caught on among some children in England and South Africa. The rules are simple. While the elves are eating, suddenly someone yells "Mush Face!" It's amazing to watch the mad scramble that follows. The elves grab their food—and everyone else's—and do all they can to get it all over the other fellow's face.

The elf who ends up with the cleanest face is the winner.

As far as Mrs. Santa is concerned, this is her least favorite elvish game.

Mrs. Santa isn't too pleased. . . .

Source:
—*Guide to Specialized Formation Flying,* U.S. Air Force Tech. Manual RS-m32/911, vol. 13.

—Interview with Manager, Creative Food Uses Division, General Foods, Inc.

Before: Suddenly someone yells "Mush Face!" and the game is on. Watch old Rhemb—he almost always wins.

During.

After: As usual, Rhemb came out untouched.

Deer Dancing

A popular game when it's especially cold outside is "Dancing the Doe-Si-Doe." In the dance, each elf chooses a reindeer partner and does a series of doe-si-does, ever trying to perfect the art.

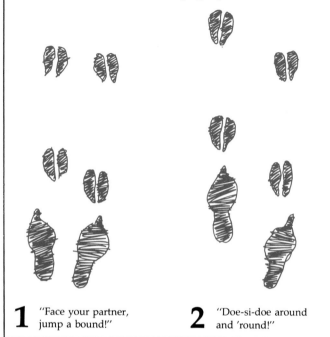

1 "Face your partner, jump a bound!"

2 "Doe-si-doe around and 'round!"

Hide and Seek. Elves play hide and seek the way everyone else does—except that they can hide anywhere! Raful, for instance, was once found in Cincinnati under a garbage can—fourteen weeks after the game started! And Fringle once hid so well that he had to go into hibernation in Mexico. The other players found him that following June.

Big ball is funnest for the elves outside the ball!

Big Ball. No one is sure who invented this game—but once the idea gets out, it will surely spread from Pole to Pole. In Big Ball, the first elf (usually selected by drawing sticks—the one with the short stick gets to go first) climbs into the ball. Then the other elves seal it up.

Don't worry—there's plenty of air in the ball!

Once the elf is comfortable in the ball, his companions start to roll it around. They roll and roll, over snowbanks, across the garden, down ice hills. When the elf inside finally starts to moan, they stop and pull him out.

The elf who can roll around the longest without moaning is the winner.

Because the ball is hollow, a few elves can move it with ease.

74

Hopscotch. The elves introduced this game to the North Pole, but now it's been adopted by Santa and Mrs. Santa. Santa first played the game in the late 1700s—and beat even the best elves. Then Mrs. Santa played him—and won! Pretty soon it had turned into a real contest, to see who could win the most times at hopscotch.

For quite a while Santa had a real winning streak. He and Mrs. Santa would play every day (except for Christmas season) and Santa won 1329 times in a row. But then Mrs. Santa changed her strategy. Now she has a slight edge on Santa. The overall score is:
Mrs. Santa—31,222
Santa—30,961

The elves dropped out of the contest quite early, since they couldn't keep up—even though they invented the game!

The taw they use in hopscotch is a candy cane. The winner of that round gets to eat it!

Source:
—Bernie Eerickson, *Games Elves Play*, Dortmund: Foundation for the Preservation of Elvish Culture, 1863.

Ice Nymphs Mean Trouble

The Ice Nymphs are furry little creatures about two feet tall. They're extremely intelligent and always come in Siamese pairs. (Legend tells of an Ice Nymph who was born singly—he was driven from their territory. After all, you can't have a one-headed nymph walking around nymph town!) Unlike most nymphs of the world, North Pole Ice Nymphs are inexplicably all male.

Shortly after Santa arrived at the North Pole, he noticed that something—or someone—was stealing his stuff. He didn't know it, but it was the nymphs. They're crafty little buggers, and when they see something they like, they find a way to get it.

Santa reacted to the thefts by putting all his stores into a single, steel-lined room. *This will keep them out,* he thought, *whatever they are.*

But the smart little nymphs put their heads together and came up with a plan. Super-hot fire will cut a hole through steel, so if they could invent an instrument to focus the fire, they'd be able to get into Santa's storeroom.

The hole didn't have to be very big, and it was easy enough to cut once they'd invented the cutting torch. (If they'd known about blow-torches it would have saved them some trouble. But it's hard to know about everything when you're isolated up at the North Pole, unless you're Santa himself!) Before long they were into the room and carrying out all the things they wanted.

Then Santa decided to bury his supplies deep under the ice. Surely the thieves couldn't get it there! But Santa didn't know that Ice Nymphs *love* to dig into ice.

Finally Santa gave up and put his supplies right on his front step. And stayed up all night to see what kind of creature came to get them. That's when he saw the Ice Nymphs for the first time. They were too fast to catch—but their Siameseness gave him an idea.

The next day Santa made a special cap. It was very warm, and very comfortable. "This will get them," he muttered. He put some more supplies on his front step, with the cap on top of them, and waited.

Shortly after midnight, the head Ice Nymph sneaked out of the shadows. His right side reached up and grabbed the cap, and cackled. "Heh-heh," he said. "Nice cap. Warm cap. Keep me warm." And he put it on his head.

But the left side snarled at him "My cap," he said. "My head is cold. I need cap." And he snatched it off his right side.

"My cap!" the right side shouted, grabbing it away.

"My cap!" the left side yelled, snatching it back.

While they were arguing, Santa crept up behind them and trapped them in his net. "*My* cap!" he said triumphantly.

That night Santa took the opportunity to teach the nymphs some manners. Since then they've been his friends. And they've never stolen from Santa again. Much.

Notes:

—The Ice Nymphs are the proud originators of the wise saying, "Two heads are better than one."

—Ice Nymphs are distant cousins to the Hairy Gorf, a member of the elvish family tree. The best way to tell the two species apart is to count them—do they come in a set or a single unit?

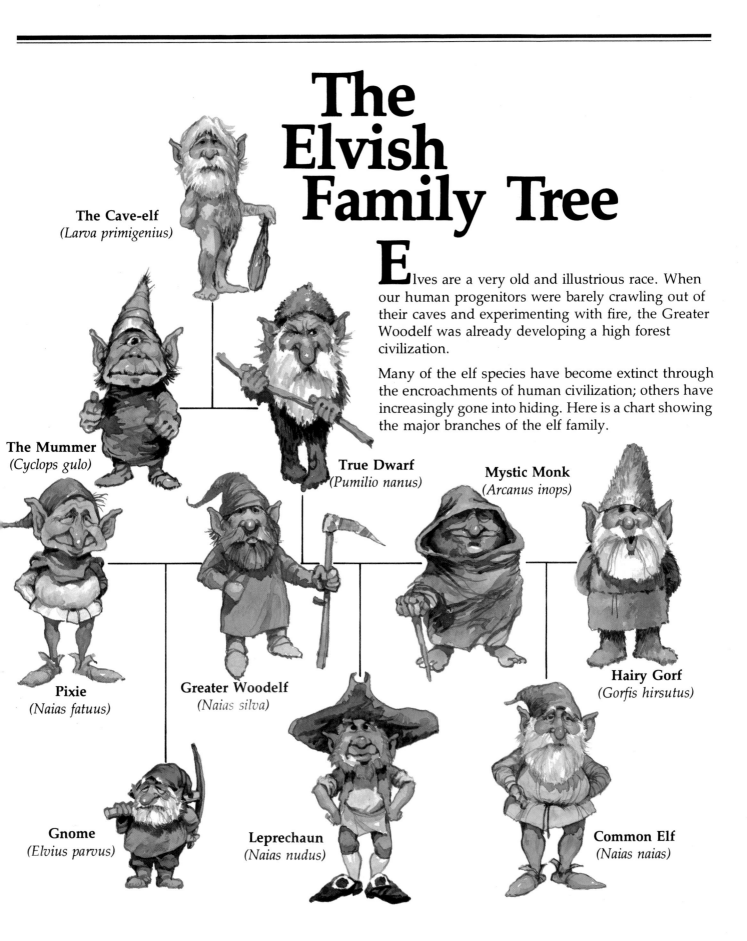

The Elvish Family Tree

Elves are a very old and illustrious race. When our human progenitors were barely crawling out of their caves and experimenting with fire, the Greater Woodelf was already developing a high forest civilization.

Many of the elf species have become extinct through the encroachments of human civilization; others have increasingly gone into hiding. Here is a chart showing the major branches of the elf family.

The Cave-elf
(*Larva primigenius*)

The Mummer
(*Cyclops gulo*)

True Dwarf
(*Pumilio nanus*)

Mystic Monk
(*Arcanus inops*)

Pixie
(*Naias fatuus*)

Greater Woodelf
(*Naias silva*)

Hairy Gorf
(*Gorfis hirsutus*)

Gnome
(*Elvius parvus*)

Leprechaun
(*Naias nudus*)

Common Elf
(*Naias naias*)

The Major Elf Species: A full record of all the branches of the elvish family tree would require volumes; the preceding page showed the relationship of only the *major* ones. Below I have given an admittedly generalized and oversimplified accounting of the most influential or most remarkable species. These pages are presented for the enlightenment of the layman; those who desire detailed descriptions of each species will have to go to the source material.

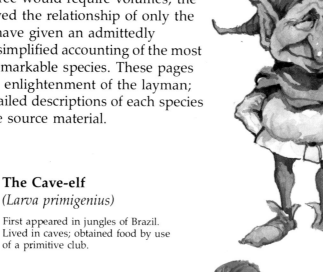

Pixie *(Naias fatuus)*

Worldly wise elf that inhabits the more temperate regions of the Western world. When caught the Pixie will assume a foolish demeanor to deceive his captors and lull them into complacency. Has highly developed sense of hearing. Is able to consume great amounts of food at a single sitting.

The Cave-elf
(Larva primigenius)

First appeared in jungles of Brazil. Lived in caves; obtained food by use of a primitive club.

Greater Woodelf
(Naias silva)

A larger cousin to the Lesser Woodelf. Inhabits hollow trees and fallen logs, if they can be cleaned. Stout and sturdy species, hard to catch and even harder to kill. Source of the legends of the immortal Mundycums of the Forest. A helpful friend to smaller animals of the brush, the Greater Woodelf is extremely suspicious of mankind.

The Mummer *(Cyclops gulo)*

One of nature's sad mistakes. Remains have been found only in the catacombs of Egypt. Apparently in the diminished light the body evolved to the point where only one eye was necessary. Although the Mummer has been virtually forgotten, one of his inventions remains: the monocle.

Mystic Monk *(Arcanus inops)*

So named because of clothing fragments that have been found, supporting earlier theories that this strain of elves placed mystical importance in robes and capes. Some anthropologists believe that all males in this race were celibates, but historical evidence suggests otherwise.

True Dwarf *(Pumilio nanus)*

An early descendant of the Cave-elf, the True Dwarf still exists in some parts of the world. Living in caves like his ancestor, the True Dwarf lives off wild berries and the meat of his enemies. Of nasty disposition. Not to be confused with descriptions of dwarves often found in mythology and popular legend.

Hairy Gorf *(Gorfis hirsutus)*

An extremely rare species of elf, currently extant in the wilds of Siberia. Hairy Gorfs are very skilled in languages; most can speak five or six tongues as well as Gorfish. Have difficulty with human languages, however. What appears to be a hat and boots are really actual hair on the Gorf's body. The Gorf wears neither hat nor boots.

Common Elf *(Naias naias)*

The Common Elf is flourishing throughout the entire world. Wherever man can be found, E. elvius can also be found. Particularly strong in the rural areas of America and Europe. This elf usually shares the house of a human, though of course without the human's knowledge. Most famous for the members of the species that serve with Santa Claus at the North Pole.

Gnome *(Elvius parvus)*

A flourishing family of elves found in virtually every part of the world. Their success at survival may be ascribed in part to the fact that they are the smallest of the elves. A fierce enemy of mice and moles, Gnomes live underground and come up only at night. Very skilled with digging and mining instruments.

A Few Other Species: Some other types of elves are here included, primarily because of their uniqueness:

Schall-oo *(Caecus clamosus)*

The Schall-oo is a native of central Asia. Just larger than a gnome, it lives under rocks in damp places. A night-creature, Schall-oos who are brought into the sunlight become totally helpless, incapacitated by the sun's brightness. Nevertheless, they've been able to survive by becoming invisible in light. (Note picture.) Schall-oos are total vegetarians; any kind of meat brings great boils into their mouths. Named for the breathing noise they make when walking.

Goblin *(Larva lamia)*

Believed to be a direct descendant of *L. primigenius*, an actual specimen of the Goblin has never been found. A picture is unavailable. Noted through legend for his evil disposition, the Goblin was reputed to have huge incisor teeth. According to the stories, more than one human has awakened after a restless night of sleep to find the marks of Goblin teeth on his throat. The famous Dracula, a Vampyre Goblin, was apparently a mutation of the species.

Black Jockey *(Agaso niger)*

This species of elf was formerly very common. They were black-skinned and wore what looked like horse-riding togs. When seen they would freeze in place, usually on lawns or by driveways, standing so still that many people mistook them for lawn ornaments. The Black Jockey preferred to live near rich people—he lived off oil droppings of cars, and the wealthy used a higher quality oil. Unfortunately, the Black Jockey is fast becoming extinct. Many have been run over by careless drivers, and others were captured in their frozen state by property owners. (Since the Black Jockey has been seen by most people, a picture is unnecessary.)

Faery *(Dryas cantus)*

Inhabits the jungles of Africa and South America, dwelling primarily in trees. The Faery is able to leap long distances from tree to tree, hence the popular belief that Faeries can fly. Many tribes of Faeries have domesticated large animals, holding a peculiar spell over them by singing in odd rhythms into their ears.

Leprechaun *(Naias nudus)*

Famed in Irish folklore, the Leprechaun has actually never inhabited Ireland. (A distant cousin has, however: the Brownie.) Leprechauns are joyful folk, always eager to laugh and ever loving a rousing dance. Their chefs are renowned among all elves, though mainly by word of mouth. On holidays their dress is similar to the American Pilgrims'; normally, however, they remain nude.

Sources:

—*A Compleat Zoology,* Dr. Adams Andrews and Dr. Margaret Andrews, New York: Scientific Publishing, Inc., 1981, 1016 pp.

—*Comparative Elvish and Dwarfish Relationships: An Historical Analysis,* Dr. Edom Lot et al., Cairo: Alkanah and Ra, 1976, 423 pp.

Telling Santa What You Want

Christmas time rolls around and everyone in the world wants to tell Santa what he or she wants. Think about it. You've had your eye on something special for quite a while. "I wish I could have that," you say to yourself. "I wish I had some money." You dream about that thing at night. When you wake up in the morning you rub your eyes and stretch—and then you remember you dreamed something important at night. What was it? You think a spell.

Then it comes back. Oh, *yes!* The thing you wish you had.

Finally there's no way out of it. You either have to ask Santa to give it to you for Christmas, or you go without.

The things people ask Santa for come in all sizes:

boat	new train
new car	coloring books
dump truck	watercolor set
new doll	to not be a klutz
new baby	doll house
new dog	new underpants
motorhome	new game
race track set	and lots of other things.
new bike	

Santa's glad to hear about all the things you want, but you should know that he can't give you everything. For example, if you want a new baby sister, don't tell Santa. Tell your mom and dad. They'll probably know how to get one.

And if you want to ask for a puppy, make sure your mom and dad approve. Puppies poop on the carpet and whine all night when people are trying to sleep. Maybe your folks will want you to have a cat instead. Cats poop in a special box and don't cause much trouble besides scratching people and climbing up the curtains and leaving fur all over and yowling at night.

When Santa gets a letter from someone, he transfers the requests for gifts onto a master list.

80

There are a lot of ways to tell Santa about what you want. The most popular way is to write him a letter. This works only for people who know how to write. If you don't know how to write, find someone to write it for you. Or you might try a Telephone Order or the Wishful Thinking Receiver. (I tell you more about those in a couple of pages.)

If you decide to write to Santa, you need to know about two problems. The first is that letters sometimes get lost in the mail. Oh, I know that *almost never* happens—after all, I've read the brochure printed by the Post Office that explains that letters are *almost never* lost in the mail.

Still I know about kids who've gotten their letters lost in the mail. One of them was Billy Wilde, who lived in North Dakota. Billy was six and was just learning to write. He was proud of the letter he sent Santa. But it got lost in the mail. Billy was scared to death he wouldn't get any presents that year. Thank heavens for the Wishful Thinking Receiver!

The second problem with writing to Santa is that he just doesn't have time to read all the letters. They start pouring in about the first of December—and that's when he's busiest getting toys ready for Christmas. When is he going to have time to read letters?

And think of how many he gets! One year he kept track of the number, just so I could put it in this book. Would you believe that Santa got 28,147,091 letters that year! It's a good thing that most kids used the Wishful Thinking Receiver instead of writing. Even Santa can't read *that* fast! He gets some elves to help him (ones that have learned to read human languages), but even then it's quite a chore.

How to Write to Santa

Here's how to write a letter to Santa that will bring results, every time:

Address the letter: Dear Santa. Don't call him Dear—

Saint Nick	Mr. Kris
Santa Claus	Mr. Kringle
St. Nicholas	Sir
Old Man	Gentlemen
Santa	Fatso
Mr. Claus	Elf-breath
Kris Kringle	

Start by buttering him up a little:
"I hope you haven't gotten a cold this year."
"Is Mrs. Claus still making that delicious plum pudding?"
"I think Rudolph looks great with a red nose!"

Here's Santa's correct address, so you'll be sure your letter gets to the right place:
Santa Claus
North Pole

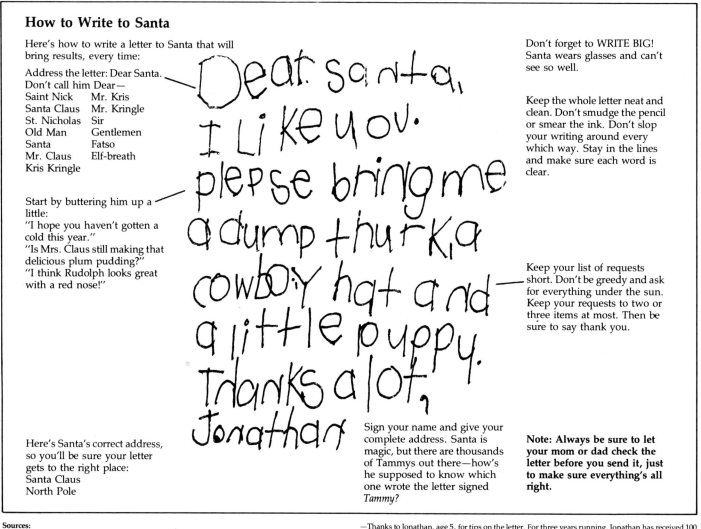

Dear santa,
I Like you.
plepse bring me
a dump thurk, a
cowboy hat and
a little puppy.
Thanks a lot,
Jonathan

Don't forget to WRITE BIG! Santa wears glasses and can't see so well.

Keep the whole letter neat and clean. Don't smudge the pencil or smear the ink. Don't slop your writing around every which way. Stay in the lines and make sure each word is clear.

Keep your list of requests short. Don't be greedy and ask for everything under the sun. Keep your requests to two or three items at most. Then be sure to say thank you.

Sign your name and give your complete address. Santa is magic, but there are thousands of Tammys out there—how's he supposed to know which one wrote the letter signed *Tammy?*

Note: Always be sure to let your mom or dad check the letter before you send it, just to make sure everything's all right.

Sources:
—Thanks to the following for their technical assistance with the information on this page:
U.S. Postal Service
Her Majesty's Royal Postal Service
Deutsche Bundpost
Transylvania Mails

—Thanks to Jonathan, age 5, for tips on the letter. For three years running, Jonathan has received 100 percent of what he asked Santa for.

Telephone Orders. Some people like to talk more than they like to write. To accommodate them, Santa has established a telephone ordering service. By using the phone ordering service, kids can call directly to the North Pole and tell Santa what they want. (Your local phone company should have the number to call from your area. But if it's not in the directory, forget it; they don't have it.)

Here's how to place your call:

1. Dial the number.

2. When the accountant mouse answers the phone, speak clearly. Tell him your name and address.

3. Next, read your Christmas list over the phone. Don't read too fast; mice write slowly.

4. Say "Thank you," and hang up.

5. Wait excitedly for Christmas!

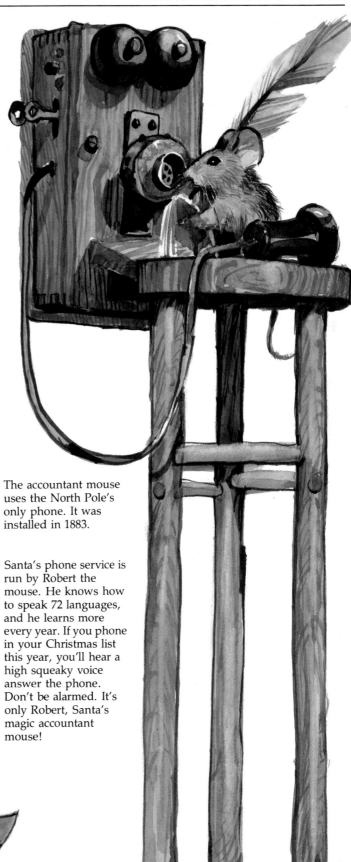

The accountant mouse uses the North Pole's only phone. It was installed in 1883.

Robert writes the message in New Mousish, Lower Dialect. He translates it for Santa's list later.

Santa's phone service is run by Robert the mouse. He knows how to speak 72 languages, and he learns more every year. If you phone in your Christmas list this year, you'll hear a high squeaky voice answer the phone. Don't be alarmed. It's only Robert, Santa's magic accountant mouse!

Source:
—Personal notes of Alexander Graham Bell, filed in Greater Manhattan Public Library, fourth floor, room 4328, Mrs. Mitchell's drawers.

To get the Wishful Thinking Receiver working for you, all you have to do is start thinking real hard!

The Wishful Thinking Receiver. A lot of kids don't know how to write, or they don't have a stamp, or they live where there isn't a post office, or they're just smart and know that Santa has to read 28,000,000 letters each year and he might not have time for theirs.

To help those kids, Santa invented the Wishful Thinking Receiver. Here's how you use it:

1. Think of what you want for Christmas.

2. Keep it a secret so the energy won't be used up. Tell only your mom or dad and brother or sister and *no one else.*

3. Think real hard about what you wish you had.

4. The Wishful Thinking Receiver will automatically pick it up.

Before Santa makes his Christmas trip each year, he looks at the list his Wishful Thinking Receiver has made for him. It has everything neatly typed up in categories, telling him how many kids in New York City want dolls and how many in Moscow want trains and how many in Johannesburg, South Africa, want worms, and so on.

If you ever take a tour of the North Pole, be sure to ask to see the Wishful Thinking Receiver. It's one of the neatest things up there.

Sources:

—Personal observations, with Author's notes, notepad 13.

—*Little-Known Inventions of the World,* unpublished manuscript, Richard Richter Reasoner, vol. 22, p. 3328.

Loading the Sleigh

The actual loading of the sleigh begins very, very early in the morning of December 23. But the sleigh crew starts many days before that: on December 12, snow or shine, the elves drag the sleigh out of its shed and haul it out into the snowy meadow. There they'll have room to work on it.

Elves don't like the cold—those who think otherwise have simply been deceived. So the sleigh crew bundles up as warm as they can get before they go out to do their work.

First layer: skin.

Next: deer tufting, taken from the hair the reindeer shed the summer before. This is applied with a paste directly to the skin.

Third layer: underclothes. Insulated.

Fourth layer: overunderclothes. Insulated. These are specially designed to hold the body heat in. (Something elves are in dire need of: their body temperature is only 69.9.)

Fifth layer: woolen shirt and pants. (Usually donated from Argentina.)

Sixth layer: sweaters and overalls.

Seventh layer: coats and hats.

Even with all their protection, the elves can stay out for only 85 minutes before they have to take a break. More than once they've proposed that they ready the sleigh inside the shed, but they can't resolve one basic problem: the ice oil they polish it with, obtained from skin excretions of the ice nymphs, will work only in the cold!

The sleigh crew begins its work by wiping the dust away with snow. Every part of the sleigh is thoroughly cleaned: body, runners, upholstery, foot rests, storage box. Then it's polished with the ice oil. Gradually it transforms from a dull, ordinary snow sled to a sleek sky-sleigh, one able to fly through the air carrying the most famous man in the world.

On December 22, fifteen elves join in and haul the sleigh over to the workshop. They take the reins out of storage and give them a good rub-down with goose grease, which makes them warm and supple. Other elves complete their preparations of the reindeer.

On December 23 the elves start loading up the sleigh. They work nonstop for nearly thirty-six hours, always finishing just before midnight on Christmas Eve!

(Every year Santa wonders out loud why the elves don't start a little sooner—"You're going to make me late one of these years," he chides them. "Every year I nearly have a heart attack from worry!"

The head elf just shrugs his shoulders and grins. He knows Santa can't have a heart attack and die, and he knows he won't make Santa late. So he isn't greatly concerned. "We don't want things to get boring," the elf says.)

Official portrait of Limlim, the first of the elves. Limlim is credited with establishing the official sleigh-loading ritual.

Loading the Sleigh includes a thousand little details—and disaster is the result if even one is overlooked. To make sure things go smoothly, the elves have devised a complex checklist to cover every aspect of preparing the sleigh for Santa's flight. Below is just a sampling of the many things that must be done.

A special mixture of oats and other grains, mixed with molasses. One final snack and the reindeer are ready for a high-speed worldwide flight.

A strong young deer named Jake. He's well-trained and is always Santa's first choice for a replacement should one of the other deer be unable to go. This year he's substituting for Comet, who has a bad case of scours. Very soon Jake will become a regular.

Tired and weak elves, part of the shift that should have gotten off an hour ago.

Reins being prepared for Cupid. Note the bells on the reins—these are used to help the reindeer fly rhythmically, in unison.

The reins must be put on with just the right amount of tension. Too tight and the reindeer won't be able to eat or even breath properly. Too loose and the deer won't be able to adequately feel Santa's directions at the other end.

Sources:

—Personal interviews with Raful, sleigh-loading foreman, and Amt, one of the trainees.

—*Elves Manual of Rules*, chapter 14, "Procedures of Preparing and Loading the Sleigh." The original manual was engraved in wood by Limlim; subsequent copies have been handwritten by the elves on ordinary paper.

—"Sleigh-loading Checklist," photocopy, in author's possession.

Santa's magic toy bag, in which the elves are able to fit gifts for every boy and girl in the world.

Very strong belt, later to be cinched tight. The belt keeps the toys from falling off the sleigh and onto someone's head. (Everyone should be in bed, anyway.)

The sleigh isn't that high,. but it's too high even for the biggest of the elves. Justa, the biggest of the elves, gets the assignment of climbing the ladder and stashing the toys into the bag. (If they tried to load the bag before they put it into the sleigh, even Santa couldn't lift it!)

Raful, foreman of the sleigh elves. Raful has just completed storing warm bricks under the seat of the sleigh, to help Santa keep warm.

A new load for the sleigh.

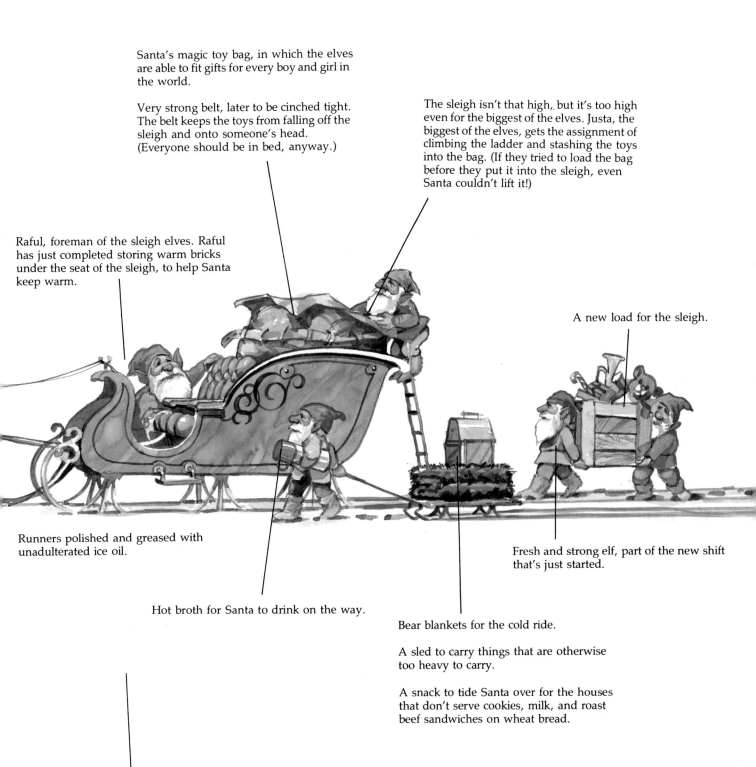

Runners polished and greased with unadulterated ice oil.

Fresh and strong elf, part of the new shift that's just started.

Hot broth for Santa to drink on the way.

Bear blankets for the cold ride.

A sled to carry things that are otherwise too heavy to carry.

A snack to tide Santa over for the houses that don't serve cookies, milk, and roast beef sandwiches on wheat bread.

Fresh snow that blew in overnight.

How Reindeer Fly

If there's anything calculated to bring disbelief to the human mind, it's the idea that reindeer can fly. One look at those shaggy, non-aerodynamically designed creatures should be enough to tell anyone with half a wit that they could never, never ever fly!

And yet they do!

They lift off clean and easy from almost any surface, skimming through the air effortlessly, light as a feather.

But that's not all. These heavy mammals, which look as if they're lucky to be able to walk around without breaking their spindly legs, *can fly faster than any other known bird or animal.* Only man's mechanical devices can do better—and they gulp unconscionable amounts of precious fossil fuels.

Because the thought that reindeer really could fly was such an unlikely idea—I frankly figured that that was one myth I'd surely disprove when I talked with Santa—when I learned it was true, I just had to have some scientific investigations.

With Santa's permission, I arranged to have a noted aero-research engineer meet me in Greenland one summer's day, when the reindeer weren't required for any North Pole duties. I brought with me one fine specimen of a reindeer, named Blitzen, who is one of the most powerful reindeer a person would ever hope to meet. The scientist, Dr. Werner Eberhardt, brought with him an impressive array of instruments.

Dr. Eberhardt checked Blitzen from horn to heel, measuring, tapping—and muttering all the while. Every once in a while he'd exclaim, "Meine Gute!" or "Gesamtlich unglaublich!"

I could hardly restrain myself, but I held my tongue until he was finished. Then I said, excited, "Well?"

He looked at me with disbelief in his eyes. "It's hard to believe," he said in his thick German accent, "but this reindeer really *can* fly!"

Dr. Eberhardt then explained that it was all in the antlers—that a reindeer's antlers were so aerodynamically designed that they could give the deer even more lift than a bird or a plane.

Comparative Speeds

Nature has produced a wide variety of flying creatures, all with different capacities and speeds. Among them, the reindeer is unsurpassed. The deer can lift faster, go higher, and maintain a greater consistent velocity then any other flying creature.

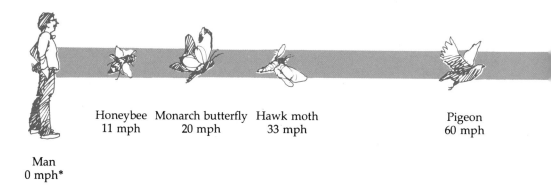

Man
0 mph*

Honeybee
11 mph

Monarch butterfly
20 mph

Hawk moth
33 mph

Pigeon
60 mph

*Note: Man cannot fly at any speed—but he sure wishes he could!

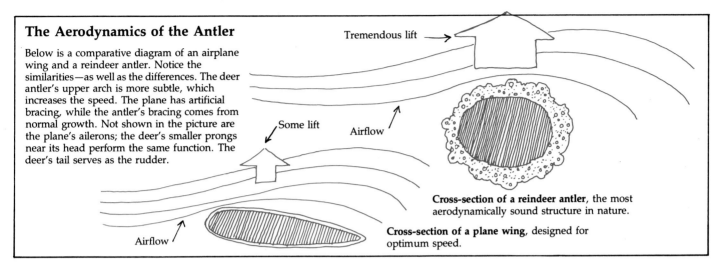

The Aerodynamics of the Antler

Below is a comparative diagram of an airplane wing and a reindeer antler. Notice the similarities—as well as the differences. The deer antler's upper arch is more subtle, which increases the speed. The plane has artificial bracing, while the antler's bracing comes from normal growth. Not shown in the picture are the plane's ailerons; the deer's smaller prongs near its head perform the same function. The deer's tail serves as the rudder.

Tremendous lift →

Some lift

Airflow

Cross-section of a reindeer antler, the most aerodynamically sound structure in nature.

Airflow

Cross-section of a plane wing, designed for optimum speed.

He then tried to get Blitzen to fly for us; but since neither of us was adept at communicating with a reindeer, Blitzen just stood there, looking like he knew something we didn't.

Finally Dr. Eberhardt gave the demonstration himself: "I'm absolutely certain they get into the air by kicking their feet together like this—" and he got down on his hands and knees, then slapped his hands and knees together. "That gives them the impetus to get going. After that—" here the good doctor put his hands to his head and wiggled his fingers—"the antlers do the rest."

"I must, absolutely *must*, write about this in our international research journal!" (Those who are interested can read the details of Dr. Werner Eberhardt's scientific findings in the *International Journal of Aerodynamic Research*, published in Bern, Switzerland, volume 63, number 11, pp. 878-943. Those who are unable to find the journal in their local library can write directly to Bern.)

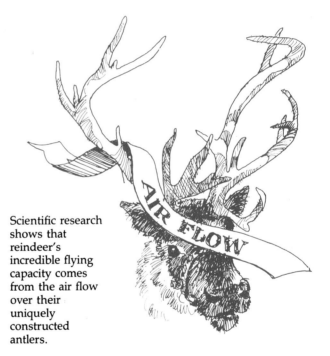

Scientific research shows that reindeer's incredible flying capacity comes from the air flow over their uniquely constructed antlers.

Spine-tailed swift
106 mph

Reindeer
clocked speed:
317 mph (believed
to go much faster)

Sources:
—Tales of the Muk-Muks, oral history, tape recording and transcript, Archives, Smithe Historical Library, Aberystwyth, Wales.
—Royal Canadian Air Force mission logs, Bldg. M, Room 4-F, "Secret" file, drawer 6.

What Happens to Nonbelievers

full head of hair

laugh wrinkles around eyes

sparkle in eyes

big smile

says "Good morning!" to people he meets

well-groomed

healthy posture

Before

going bald

eyes dull and lifeless

frown wrinkles around eyes and nose

smelly

frown around mouth

says "Bah, Humbug!" to people he meets

clothes dirty and unkempt

shuffles as he walks

After

It's strange but true: some people don't believe there is a Santa Claus. It's hard to explain why. But when a person stops believing, some very sad things begin to happen.

Shown here is a Before and After picture of the same person, to demonstrate what happens to nonbelievers. The person who believed (Before) was happy and healthy. But when he stopped believing (After), he began to suffer from the Scrooge Syndrome. He quickly went downhill, and, if he's typical, he'll die much younger than the believer. (The second picture was taken only two weeks after the first!)

Sources:

—*Annual Report of the Surgeon General of the United States*, 1959, in Archives, Library of Congress, Washington, D.C.

—"Symposium on the 'Scrooge Syndrome,'" Cambridge Symposia Series, 1911, reported in *British Lancer*, 123:10:400-439.

Quick As a Wink

A wink is one of the fastest things known to man (it takes only .01 of a second!), yet that's how fast Santa must deliver his toys to each house. Figure it out for yourself—in one night he must travel around the world, making millions of stops; and he only has from 10 p.m. (when the kids go to bed) to 5 a.m. (when the kids wake up) to do it in!

But Santa can be incredibly fast. In quick succession, he lands his sleigh on the rooftop, drops down the chimney, leaves the packages by the tree, eats the cookies left for him, drinks the milk, puts his finger by his nose, and pops back up the chimney. Santa's used to quickness—it doesn't even leave him out of breath!

1
First, Santa comes down the chimney. (Or he gets into the house however he can. One sly homeowner once saw him entering through the drainpipe!)

2
Next, Santa rushes to the tree and leaves the gifts.

3
He eats the cookies and milk—or stuffs it into his vest to eat it later.

4
And then he rises back up the chimney, his finger placed delicately on the side of his nose.

91

A Very White Christmas

It's easy to fall into a comfortable routine and never change it. That's what Santa was doing with his Christmas deliveries—every year it was the same. That was good enough for him. But Mrs. Santa's handmaiden got tired of it one year, and decided she was going to make a change.

"This year we're going to have a themed Christmas," she announced one morning, late in October. "And I'm in charge."

Santa's a jolly old fellow—he likes people to be happy. So he figured he'd let the handmaiden do her thing. After all, what harm could it do?

The handmaiden began planning right away. "Things are really going to be different this year," she said gleefully. "People are getting tired of the same old thing."

She tried to gather ideas from the elves, but they weren't much help. And she didn't know how to talk to the reindeer. Santa and Mrs. Santa were too busy to share ideas. "But that's all right," the handmaiden said to herself. "I can be creative when I need to."

Late one night in November, just before Thanksgiving, she burst into Santa's cottage. "I've got it!" she shouted. "I've got it!"

Santa and Mrs. Santa looked up politely. "Yes?"

"We'll have a white Christmas this year. A very white Christmas. A very, *very* white Christmas. You'll love it!" And she left without another word.

Santa looked at Mrs. Santa and winked. "It will be all right, Mama," he said.

The next morning the handmaiden was up early, already at work on her plan. She painted the sleigh white. She bleached Santa's Christmas clothes white, and whitened his gift bag. She spray-painted the reindeer, and their antlers, and their reins.

Every day she worked on her plan. When the elves started to wrap the gifts in the regular wrapping paper, she stopped them, horrified. "No," she shouted at them. "Only *white* paper will do!" And she promptly gave them white paper to wrap the gifts in. "This is going to be a very white Christmas," she said proudly.

It all seemed innocent enough. When one of the elves complained, Santa smiled kindly. "Oh, what does it hurt?" he asked.

But that was before Christmas Eve. Santa got a late start because he couldn't find his sleigh, camouflaged in the snow. When he finally took off, the weather was bad. It was next to impossible for the reindeer to remain stable in the blizzardy snow.

Finally Santa had to make a forced landing. Off in the winter wilderness, somewhere.

Because Santa and the sleigh and the reindeer were all white, it took the elvish rescue party two days to even find them. And then they had to use sled dogs to smell them out. Christmas didn't come until December 29 that year—and then it was a very, very *red* Christmas. Santa had seen to that! And they've never had a themed Christmas since!

The elves and sled dogs
searched for two days to find
Santa and his sleigh. But it
was pretty hard to see the
white Santa in the midst of the
white snow!

Why Rudolph's Nose Is Red

The Great North Wind is usually quite peaceful. He'll go his way and let you go yours. But every once in a while he gets totally fed up with the human race. He gets tired of sharing the air with airplanes and balloons and rockets and kites. "I'm going to get rid of them," he roars. "And I'm going to get rid of all the people who make them, too!"

When the Great North Wind gets like that, watch out! He'll blow and blow until he blows your brains out, if he can!

One year Santa and the elves were working hurriedly, trying to get ready for Christmas. It seemed that everything was going wrong—and Christmas Eve was getting closer and closer.

Then the bad got worse for them. One by one, they all got the flu—Santa, then the elves, then the reindeer. For a while Mrs. Santa treated them with her powerful home remedies. But the remedies weren't strong enough. And then she got the flu, too.

It was a sorry state of affairs. Here everything was behind schedule, and no one had the strength to work.

Then the worse got even more worse! Because about that time the Great North Wind decided to throw a tantrum. "I'm sick of it!" he bellowed. (The Great North Wind finds it impossible to talk nicely, even when he's in a good mood.) "I'm going to get them all!" he shouted. And he began to get ready to attack all of the men and women and children on earth.

The reindeer were in their stables when the Great North Wind roared out his threat, and they shivered with the power of it. "We must warn Santa," they whispered. "He must know about this!"

So they went in to see Santa, and told him in sign language what they'd heard. "This is serious," Santa said, sitting feebly in his bed, "very serious indeed!" He stroked his beard, his hand pale. "We must warn the people of the world. Who can we send? I'm too sick. All the elves are sick. Are any of the reindeer well enough to fly?"

At first Rudolph had to wear dark glasses to protect his eyes from the bright light of his nose—and so did everyone else. But now they're used to it!

"Only one," was the answer. "Young Rudolph."

"Then we must send him," Santa said. "I'll write a message and he can deliver it to the people of the world."

That night Rudolph took off on his solitary flight. He had barely begun when the Great North Wind saw him flying through the air. "Arrgh," the Great North Wind growled. "An enemy! I'll destroy him!" And he sent a bolt of lightning down onto Rudolph.

It was too much for the tiny deer to withstand. The electricity of the lightning passed through his body, causing his heart to stop. His body shuddered, then died, and he fell, down, down toward the earth.

"Arrgh!" the Great North Wind shouted. "I got him!" And he sent another lightning bolt after Rudolph's limp form.

Again the electrical current passed through his body—and it started his heart again! Rudolph came back to life, and quickly resumed his flight.

But a strange thing happened. The electrical charge remained in him, and his nose began to glow, brighter and brighter, until even the Great North Wind couldn't bear to look at its brilliance. With his nose shining the way before him, Rudolph safely made his way through the Great North Wind's terrible storm and warned the people of the world to stay indoors until the wind was gone.

When Rudolph returned to the North Pole, some of the younger reindeer mocked him. "Hah, hah!" they said. "Red nose, red nose!" But Santa proclaimed Rudolph a hero, and let him retire from sleigh duty for life—except when the Great North Wind arises!

The Brightness of Rudolph's Nose

Rudolph's nose is truly a scientific wonder. Before he got struck by lightning twice, both times in mid-air, theoretical researchers hypothesized that such an occurrence would cause the nose to shine—but not until Rudolph did the theory become fact.

It's difficult to measure the brilliance of such a light, but through careful testing I was able to determine that Rudolph's nose is more than 35 million candle-powers bright! Fortunately, he has learned how to control the glow, so that normally you can't even tell that it's shining at all!

Source:
—*The Illuminati Papers,* author unknown, sections 3 and 7. These papers tell of ancient sources of light, both spiritual and physical.

Why There Are Fake Santas

Many years ago, in the faraway land of Cathay, there lived a prince who hated Santa Claus. He was a jealous and ugly man, and whenever he heard of Santa, he flew into a rage. "How dare you mention that man's name!" he would shout. "He's a fraud! He wants people to love and esteem him, but deep inside he's mean and stingy."

This prince told these lies because he wanted people to love and respect him—and he knew they loved Santa instead. He wanted his subjects to think he was a great prince. But everywhere he went, the people said to him, "You're just mean and ugly. You oppress us; you take instead of give. Why can't you be more like Santa Claus?"

But the prince didn't want to change. He wanted to get rid of Santa.

Finally, in desperation, he started to develop an evil plan. He would totally discredit Santa—and then people wouldn't let Santa come to their homes anymore. Then they'd have no choice—they'd have to look to their prince for their needs. Instead of the horrid Santa Claus.

The next day the prince dressed up in Santa clothes. He put on a red suit with black boots and a white beard. He put on a white wig and a red hat. Then he walked out into the town.

"Hey, look, there's Santa!" a child cried. Everyone crowded around the prince.

"We love you, Santa," the people said. "We're so glad you came to our town!"

The prince sneered at them. "You're a bunch of stupids," he said. "You're begging around me all the time. I can't stand you. I spit on you." And he spat on them.

The people were confused. Then angry. They began to chase the prince out of the town. "Don't you dare show your face around here ever again, Santa!" they shouted.

The prince gloated in his success. He'd tricked the people into hating Santa.

The next day he went into another town—and again fooled the people.

But on the third day, when he went into a third town, he was met by a very intelligent little boy. "You're not Santa," the boy said, poking his finger up into the prince's tummy.

"Of course I'm Santa!" the prince shouted. "Now get away, you little brat." He tried to push past the boy to where a crowd of other people were standing.

But the boy held his ground. "Santa doesn't have red hair sticking out from under his white hair," the boy said. "And his beard is real!"

The crowd looked closer. "He's right," they murmured. "The little boy is right!"

Suddenly they surged forward to where the prince was standing. Before he could escape, they'd knocked him to the ground and stripped off his hat and his hair and his beard and his boots and his red suit of clothes.

Then they gasped, amazed. "It's the prince," the little boy whispered.

They drove the prince out of their town; and then all the towns gathered together and drove him out of the country.

The prince moved far away and raised many sons. When the sons learned of the mean things their father had done to Santa Claus, they were horrified. "We must undo this bad thing," they said. So they began to dress up like Santa and do wonderful, loving things for other people.

The sons had sons and their sons had sons. Now there are thousands of them, all around the world. Every December they dress up like Santa and try to help other people. It's one of the nicest things there is about Christmas!

Spotting a Fake Santa. Even though fake Santas are wonderful men, it's good to know the real one from a fake. Fake Santas will have one or all of the signs shown at right. Just one sign is enough to tell you if it's the real Santa or not. But be polite, even if you know it's a faker. He's one of Santa's official helpers!

The Ten Danger Signals:

1
says "Ho! Ho! Ho!" too frequently or in a high, whiny voice

2
has brown or black or red or blond hair poking out from under a white wig

3
wears red rouge on his cheeks

4
wears a fake beard (pull on it if you're not sure)

5
is skinny—or at least not roly-poly fat

6
wears a cheap red suit, instead of a heavy one woven out of wool or elf hair

7
wears a black vinyl belt, instead of leather

8
has on white gloves over skinny fingers

9
pants are loose-fitting and are made of cotton or polyester, instead of Red Wooger

10
has on black galoshes, rubber boots, or shiny vinyl boots, instead of heavy dull-black leather ones

Source:
—*Great Imposters in Retail Merchandising*, Business Records Incorporated, 1982. Available in most retail record stores.

How Santa Gets All Those Toys into the Bag

It was the biggest accident since Blitzen fell into the chocolate vat. But I didn't know it would happen. Honest! You see, the problem started when I got curious about Santa's bag. I wanted to know just how it worked.

Bad decision. I should have just asked. But instead I stuck my big nose in the wrong place and opened the bag.

Ka-BOOM, Ker-PLOOY! The whole thing blew apart, smashing me and the bag and the toys and everything else that was around clear into the next snowbank!

I've learned since that the inside of the bag occupies a place beyond both time and space. It's like a little black hole: Santa can pack a thousand miles worth of stuff into one tiny square inch.

I've also learned not to stick my nose where it doesn't belong!

The bag has an incredible capacity. But beware! Only Santa should open it!

Why Santa Gives Lumps of Coal

There once was a little boy named George Greeley. George started out okay—but somewhere he started to get the idea that he should be given anything (and everything) he wanted. That's when things started to go bad for little George.

By the time George was eight years old, he had a new name: Greedy George Greeley. When he went to school, the other kids would greet him, "Hello, Greedy George Greeley. How are you today, Greedy George Greeley?"

Greedy George always tried to get the things that belonged to the other kids. He wouldn't steal, of course—Greedy George wasn't dishonest. He was just, well . . . **greedy!** So he'd beg. "Can I have that pencil? Huh? Huh? Can I please? Please give me your pencil—you have two nice ones and I haven't any."

When the other kid would finally break down and give Greedy George one of his pencils, George still wanted more. "That other pencil you have there sure is nice. It sure would be nice if I had a set of them. Will you give it to me? Huh? Huh?"

George got greediest of all at Christmastime. The first year he wrote a letter to Santa: "Please give me these ten items," he said. Santa wanted to please George, so he gave him as many as he could.

Greedy George got all the presents he asked for—and he still wanted more!

The next year, George sent another letter: "I want thirty-two things for Christmas. Here's a list."

"That's sure a lot of things George Greeley is asking for," Santa thought. "I can't possibly give him thirty-two. I hope he'll be satisfied with twenty-five. I don't want him to think old Santa is stingy or anything."

The next year George sent a letter that was so fat it took *five* stamps! "Dear Santa," it said. "You didn't give me everything I wanted last year. It made me real sad. I cried all Christmas day, and all the next day too. I know you don't like children to be sad. Please bring me these 112 toys this year and I'll feel better."

That's when Santa realized George Greeley wasn't just plain George Greeley anymore. He'd turned into Greedy George.

"I'm going to give that twerp a lump of coal this year!" Santa said. "Take him 112 toys! The nerve! Humph!" (Even Santa gets upset sometimes.)

That year Santa didn't take a single toy to Greedy George Greeley. All he gave him was one dirty lump of coal. "Maybe that will cure Greedy George of his greediness," Santa said to himself.

And it did! The next year George sent a letter to Santa: "Please, if you will, dear Santa, give me this one toy this Christmas." Santa smiled to himself and gave George two toys that year. And George was never greedy again.

George lived long ago, but children still get too greedy sometimes. All they think about is themselves. All they worry about is what they're going to get for Christmas. They never think about other kids. They never try to make sure that other kids will have happy Christmases too.

When a kid turns into a Greedy George, Santa knows just how to snap him out of it. On Christmas Eve, Santa leaves only one thing: a big, fat, black, and dirty lump of coal!

Finally Santa realized that George was just *greedy!* So he gave George a lump of coal.

Source:
—Letter from the American Bituminous Coal Association, in Author's possession.
—Untitled research paper on the use of lumps of coal in history, by Ruthie Johnson, Tuba City, Texas, 1969.

Why Santa Goes Down Chimneys

Many years ago Santa liked to secretly leave gifts for children. He'd sneak into their houses at night and leave presents on the hearth; in the morning they'd be surprised to find a new toy or new sweater or new something waiting for them.

Back in those days no one ever locked his house. In fact, locks hadn't been invented yet, because stealing hadn't been invented either.

It was easy enough for Santa to get in.

But then the unthinkable happened. It all started with the coal miners, and it makes one of the saddest tales in this book.

Every year the people went into the forests to get wood for their fires in the winter. And each year there was less and less wood to burn. Finally it was almost gone. "We've got to start getting coal instead," the people said.

That's how they began to make mines. Down they dug, down and down, farther and farther into the bowels of the earth. They brought up huge chunks of coal, which the people then burned in their fireplaces to keep warm.

But there was never enough coal. So the miners dug even deeper.

One day, as they were digging, they pushed their shovels into the earth—and the shovels didn't stop. They went right through, into a tremendous hole on the other side. One of the workers fell through the hole. They could hear his cry for help, far, far away. He fell and fell. They never saw him again.

There on the other side of the hole was the richest vein of coal they'd ever seen. They chipped some coal out, and that night when they went back up to the village, they showed the townspeople what they'd found. "And there's tons more of it down there, too!" they exclaimed.

That night there was a great celebration. The people knew they'd be warm for one more winter.

But the next morning, when the miners went down into the mine, the hole was gone. "Maybe it crumbled in," one of the miners said. It took them all day to clean the hole out again, and they didn't have time to get any coal out. But at least it was ready for the next day.

But the next day the hole was filled in again. "This is most curious," the foreman said. They cleared out the hole. Then they set up a strong frame to hold the dirt in the opening firm.

The next morning they noticed that the frame had been sawed on and hammered on. But the hole was still there. And now they could begin their mining.

Deep, deep in the bowels of the earth lived a group of earth trolls. They were short, stumpy creatures, with knobby skin and huge eyes to let them see in the dark. These earth trolls hated the light—and when the miners accidentally opened one of their burrows, light streamed into all of their caverns. The trolls were furious. That night, when they could see better, they patched up the hole. Then the miners opened the hole again—and the trolls closed it again. And they were getting madder and madder.

The frame was the last straw. Trolls work with earth, not with wood, and they couldn't cut the frame. All day the light poured down the mine tunnel and into the trolls' home.

"All right, that's it!" said the head troll. "We've got to put a stop to this!"

"I'm really bugged at those humans," said his assistant. "They think they own the earth."

"I've had enough of this," said the head troll's wife, blinking her big black eyes. "I can't see to bake my troll-bread and my kids cry all the time because the light hurts their eyes."

"Let's go up and kill them all!" said one.

"Let's go up and teach them a real lesson!" said another.

"Let's go up and destroy all their lights!" said a third. (All this was in troll language, of course.)

That last idea is the one that caught on. "If we destroy all their lights," the head troll said, "they won't be able to see to mine. And they can't make that awful hole anymore!"

That night the trolls poured forth from the mine tunnel. They carried their crude but horrible weapons, clutched tightly in their horny hands. When they attacked, everyone was asleep—and by midnight the trolls had won their victory.

They rounded up everyone in the town square. "These are the new rules," said the head troll, brandishing a black whip. "And you must obey them because we are your new masters.

"First, no more digging into our holes.

"Second, no more using lights in your mining; lights hurt our eyes.

"Third, you may have lights in your houses at night. But you must cover up your windows and bar your doors. If any light escapes, we'll punish you severely." He snapped the whip against the ground. "You must begin by boarding the windows tonight."

In their search for coal, the miners delved deeper and deeper into the earth. Little did they know that a tribe of trolls lived down there!

The term **Dark Ages** refers to the many, many years when the trolls reigned supreme. The Age of Enlightenment began when the trolls were trapped in the earth and ordered never to come out again.

The trolls had returned to their holes before dawn, but the people were deathly afraid of them, and they dared not disobey. They kept the three rules religiously. Months went by, and they didn't see any of the horrible trolls. Then, one night, the trolls invaded their houses, knocking down the doors, dowsing their lights, and marching them out to the town square. "We just wanted to make sure you remembered who's boss," the head troll told them.

That Christmas, Santa trudged into town through the snow. All was dark and quiet. He couldn't see a light anywhere. He went up to the first house. The door was bolted shut. The next house was locked too. The windows were boarded up. *How strange!* Santa thought. *Now how in the world am I going to leave these gifts for the children?*

Then the answer came: go down through the chimney! And that's what he's done ever since—even though no one has seen a troll for many years now.

To be able to make it around the world in one night, Santa must go down the chimney, distribute the gifts (neatly, of course!), and be back up on the roof in less than one minute! Sometimes he takes an elf with him to help him get his speed up.

The timing elf uses a watch that was given to Santa by the president of Switzerland! The casing is made of pure beaten gold.

Sources:
—Legends and tales oft repeated during shop meetings of the United Mine Workers of America.
—*Dictionary of the Dark Ages*, Old Delhi: Brilliante Publishers, 1754, p. 312.

104

About the North Pole

No one knows for sure where the North Pole came from; it's just been there ever since the world was. The pole itself is made of petrified wood and a volcanic alloy of iron and granite. It stands thirty-two feet high and is thirty-two inches in diameter. The base of the pole is firmly embedded in heavy ice.

For centuries scientists have tried to discover the secrets of Stonehenge, the Easter Island statues, and the Andean "airstrips," not to mention the Great Pyramid of Cheops. But none of these is in any way comparable to the wonderful North Pole. The pole is of much finer design, much more impressive construction, and much greater natural beauty than any of the other mysteries of ancient times.

Nearly a millennia ago, the Chinese invented the first compass. It was at that point that man recognized the secret powers that came from the very topmost point of the earth. And that's the point where the North Pole stands.

The North and South Poles act as the points on a gyroscope, keeping the earth in balance.

The elf sitting by the pole shows how big it actually is.

Occasionally the earth wobbles on its axis. To keep it in proper alignment, Santa installed a special adjusting wire on the North Pole, which he pulls when needed.

The North Pole is the pivotal spot of the earth. It's around that point that the globe revolves. The pole acts like the stem on a gyroscope, holding the earth firm and steady as it spins around and around.

How Santa Got to the North Pole. By now it's well known that Santa didn't always live at the North Pole. But many people don't know exactly how it was that he got there.

Santa began his northward trek when he was living for a time in Persia. While in Persia, he had a dream where he saw himself standing by a pole, far to the north. While he gazed at the pole, a voice came to him and said, "There is where you'll find your greatest power and blessing." Then he woke up.

Night after night the dream came to him, and finally he could ignore it no longer. Santa consulted the wisest Persian seers, but they were unable to help him understand the dream. At last he set off anyway, seeking to find the strange pole that he knew was part of his destiny. He didn't know where to find it—but he did know it was in the north.

He traveled to Turkey, and there talked with a prophet. But the prophet knew nothing of the pole.

He continued north, moving into Thrace and through the land of the Bulgarians. For a while he lived in Buda and Pest in eastern Europe, consulting the magicians and sorcerers, trying to find someone with knowledge of the pole to the north. No one could help him.

Then he turned west, making his journey to Mecklenburg, Kaupang, and Hammerfest, and from there to the islands of Spitsbergen. Finally, in the northernmost reaches of the wastelands of Greenland, he found an old holy man who lived in a hut. "I've been waiting for you," the holy man said. "Now—if you would reach the north pole, go directly north. Always north. And you will surely find it."

The journey was long and hard. But his fate drove him on. And find it he did, because the old man's vision was true!

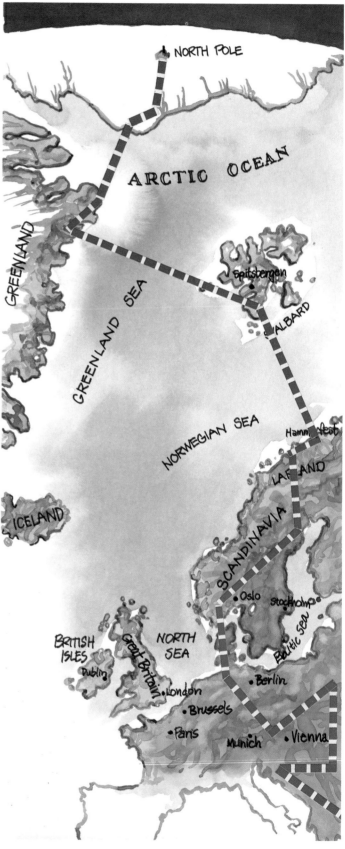

Santa's journey to the North Pole took over ten years, a long and solitary trek.

Neat Things at the North Pole

When you visit the North Pole, there are certain things you absolutely *must* see. Of course you'll want to see Santa's house and Elf Hall and all that normal stuff.But, in addition, be sure you don't miss these:

Ezra's nose was used as a model for a popular shake-and-see toy.

The snow line on the two-level house usually hits right below the top front door.

The wart on Ezra the elf's nose. Look closely and you'll see a village scene inside it. When he jumps up and down vigorously, then stops, you can see snow falling around the village.

The two-level house. When the snow gets so deep that the elves can't get in on the ground floor, they walk directly to the second-floor entrance! In fact, the winter lasts so long at the North Pole that they use the second-floor entrance more often than they do the first.

Turtle Rock, which is usually found in the bay. The rock is shaped like a turtle—and seems to be moving south at the rate of about five miles a year. Elves love to slide down the Turtle Rock—and you can try it too!

While you're near Turtle Rock, take a minute and enjoy the smells of the North Pole. Often wafting through the air is the delicious aroma of Mrs. Santa's cooking. During stable-cleaning time, you'll get a real noseful! But the best smell is the smell of excitement during Christmastime.

The giant's footprint. Left by a prehistoric giant, this footprint has been filled with water, forming a bottomless pool. It's believed to be shark-infested, so be careful!

The giant who left this footprint has never been seen. Just hope you're not the first to meet him!

Legend says that the giant who made this print was named Omar.

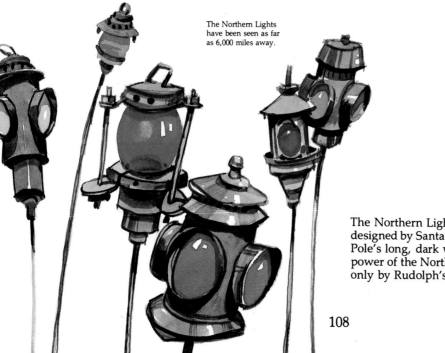

The Northern Lights have been seen as far as 6,000 miles away.

The Northern Lights, which were designed by Santa during one of the North Pole's long, dark winters. The candle power of the Northern Lights is exceeded only by Rudolph's nose.

108

The interior of the outhouse, which is decorated in early Egyptian. Some elves have become quite proficient in ancient hieroglyphics as they have studied the outhouse walls day after day.

Other things to do. In addition to the places I've listed, you'll really enjoy these other special North Pole attractions:

Take a ride on one of the reindeer. If it will let you.

Ride in the sleigh—and not just on the ground, either. But make sure Santa's doing the steering. If you go up with the elves you might come back down without the sleigh!

Visit the Polar Dragon's lair. But don't go in—just take a good sniff or two.

See if you can spot the Ice Nymphs. The best way is to entice them with something to swipe from you.

Visit the hidden cottage in the woods. An old troll is said to live there, but he only comes out at night. (Make sure you don't get caught in the forest after dark!)

Taste some of the North Pole snow. If you eat it right after it has fallen, it will taste like sugar!

Get permission to take a look at Santa's special invention collection. The Water-Maker, which distills fresh water from the air, and the Lee-Lee, a self-propelled dogsled, are especially interesting.

Encourage the elves to play a round of Mush-Mush, and watch the fun!

Get Rudolph to shine his nose so bright. But don't look directly at it—it will damage your eyes!

Eat one of Mrs. Santa's cookies. Or two, if you want to make a pig of yourself.

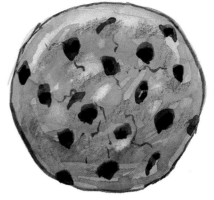

The Village

Official flag.

Lookout tower. Used mainly for sighting polar bears. (Bob the polar bear is all right, but Henry and the others like elves a little *too* much!)

The hangar. The reindeer are kept here until it's time for them to take off on Christmas Eve.

When I first arrived at the North Pole, I was halfway expecting a bunch of igloos. After all, ice *is* plentiful up there. If not igloos, then maybe some little huts huddled together in the middle of a barren wasteland.

Underground sauna and recreation area. This spa has been constructed to accommodate over 300 elves at once—or 65 humans.

Santa's cottage. Constructed over 450 years ago, the cottage has held up incredibly well. The newer addition on the side is where Santa put his laughing room.

Turtle Rock. It's usually found in the bay, but it keeps moving around.

North Pole snow. The snow at the North Pole village is somehow whiter than snow elsewhere in the world.

The enchanted forest. All forests at the North Pole are enchanted.

110

Whatever I expected, it sure wasn't what I saw! Here was a beautiful little village nestled among the trees of the forest, a village with everything a person would ever need to keep him happy. I ran from building to building like a little kid, excited to see everything at once. I peeked in the windows of Santa's cottage, sweated in the underground sauna, climbed up onto the lookout tower—and that was only the beginning!

To give you an idea of what the North Pole village looks like, I've included a picture here. This isn't all the village—many more things can be seen if you continue south. But I've been able to include most of the important things.

No one is sure who lives here, but a light is often seen at night.

Elf cottages. Elves have an incredibly strong grouping instinct, so Santa built all their cottages in a cluster. The tallest cottage is the Elf Hall, where they hibernate.

The runway. Santa uses this runway both for take-offs and landings.

Guest cottages. I stayed in the one at the right.

The North Pole. The Pole is the exact center of the village. Santa and the elves often meet here for special festivals.

Giant's footprint. This print is from the right foot. The print from the left foot has been seen at the South Pole.

Production plant and warehouse. Here's where most of the real work goes on—not counting Mrs. Santa's kitchen.

Secret hideout.

Reindeer barn. The deer are kept here when they aren't grazing the North Pole tundra. The lean-to roofs are attached to let the deer go outside without getting snowed on.

The nerve center. Here is where most of the creative thinking goes on.

The North Pole Schedule

There's always something going on at the North Pole. One minute things seem to be calm and steady, and the next minute you find you're in the middle of an elvish surprise party. Or the Ice Nymphs have stolen your pants. Or you wake up and discover it's Scare-the-Wits-Out-of-All-Guests Day—which included me!

Because Santa and the elves love so much to have fun, the yearly schedule of the North Pole gives them lots of time for parties and celebrations. But then there's a lot of work, too. Here's how the North Pole year goes:

At the Toboggan Party, everyone gets to be involved!

January 1 Elves settle down for hibernation

January 15 Polar Dragon Day—the dragon gets to move about freely for a full day

February 28 Annual Snow Ball—all inhabitants of the North Pole invited (see next page)

March 5 Yearly Snoring Contest—reindeer place bets on which elf will snore loudest during a ten-minute period

March 18 Santa begins design of new toys; produces working models

April 12 North Pole Polishing and Adjustment Day

May 31 Secret Birthday Party—Santa and Mrs. Santa enjoy a private party before the elves awaken

June 1 Elves wake up from hibernation

June 17-23 No-Night Week

July 18 Elves begin production of new toys

July 19 Elves begin summer holiday

August 1 All Fools' Day (postponed from April 1 so the elves can enjoy it too!)

September 10 Sticky-Sticky Day—Santa always begins the day with the biggest stick

October 12 Toboggan Party, held near Turtle Rock

November 30 Reindeer Formation Flying

December 12 Preparation of the sleigh begins

December 24 Christmas Eve—Santa begins his rounds

December 25 Christmas, the best day of the whole year!

Why They're Called Reindeer

Some people think reindeer are named reindeer because they wear reins when they pull Santa's sleigh—but that's a faulty linguistic back-formation.

The real truth of the matter is this: When reindeer fly too high, the clouds get hooked onto their antlers. Then, when the deer drop down to lower altitudes, the moisture in the clouds condenses, forms into water droplets, and rains onto the deer's head.

If we were going to be truly accurate, we would refer to the deer as raindeer.

Note: Some of the simpleminded, on learning the true name of reindeer, have assumed they're the mystical source of rain. I'm assured by by meteorologist friends, however, that this isn't the case.

It's not uncomfortable for a deer to get clouds stuck on his antlers. Until they start to drip on him.

Nine Reindeer

Zoologist Umi !Ku'i was the first to notice a surprising phenomenon about reindeer: in some ways they're just like chickens. Put a group of chickens together and they immediately start to establish a pecking order. The strongest chicken pecks the next strongest, which pecks the next, and on down the line. The weakest chicken of all gets pecked by everybody.

Reindeer have a hard time pecking. But they do have their own version of this peculiar custom. It's called antler order—the strongest reindeer shoves the next strongest around with his antlers, and so on, down to the weakest.

Santa's relatively civilized reindeer try to be polite in their antler order, but they have it just the same. And sometimes they're downright cruel, as they were with poor Rudolph before he saved their necks. (Now Rudolph is at the head of the antler order line—his red nose gives him quite a bit of authority.)

When I went to learn more about the reindeer, I intended to have a good look at all of them. Or at least at the "typical" ones. Unfortunately, the antler order got in the way. Whenever I'd try to interview one of the deer, using interpreting elves with their sign-language techniques, the strongest ones would always get in the way. I'd start to ask a question of one of the weaker deer, and suddenly I'd be face to face with one of the more prominent ones.

Finally I gave it up. It was no use. So here I'm giving you a look at the top nine reindeer. I admit it's not a very representative sample, but what's a fellow to do when he's faced with a snorting buck that *insists* on being interviewed first?

Rudolph is now the most prominent of all the deer. Here he's shown wearing his Elf Medal of Honor, awarded after he saved everyone at the North Pole.

Note: For more details on Rudolph, see "Why Rudolph's Nose Is Red," pp. 94-96.

Rita is presently preoccupied with her new calf. In fact, she's been so busy that she forgot the yearly formation flying!

When I visited Miko he was busy reading his number one favorite book by Shakesdeere, *King Deer.*

Rita

Rita has been around surprisingly long for a reindeer—more than 260 years. (But realize that the North Pole helps reindeer stay young and healthy, too!)

Rita is most commonly known by her nickname, Dasher—she got it by being the fastest deer fifteen years running in the annual formation-flying contest.

Last year Rita was grounded, at least temporarily. She was big with calf, and the little one was born at the beginning of this last spring. Blitzen claims to be the father, but Rita neither admits nor denies it. This calf, named Fritz, is Rita's thirty-second. Other calves born to Rita include Kyno, who was the first reindeer *ever* to step on Santa's foot, and Hhrin, popularly known as Comet.

Miko

Clement Moore did exhaustive research before he wrote his classic poem "The Night Before Christmas," and the poem is mostly accurate. But there were a few gaps in his information, and all he could do was fake it. For instance, his personal diary reveals that he was unable to obtain the correct name of Santa's second sleigh deer. His solution: he called the deer Dancer, because it rhymed with Prancer, the next deer.

The deer's real name is Miko—and he doesn't even like to dance. But perhaps Miko himself is really to blame for the problem. He's so busy reading that he hardly even looked up enough to talk to me. (Although he was true to his antler order: he wouldn't let me move on to someone else until he was darn good and ready.)

A reading reindeer is highly unusual, and Miko interrupted his reading to proudly inform me through the interpreting elf that he taught *himself*. He has since taught some of the younger generation as well.

Some of Miko's favorite books: *Rise and Fall of the Reindeer Empire, Tales of Sorrowful Deer, Moby Deer, Bambi, The Great White Stag, The Romance of John Deer and Deer Abby.*

Source:
—Rita Rhit, *Famous Ritas of History,* New York: self-published, n.d. 66 pp.

Source:
—Miko, *Guide to Teaching Reindeer Reading,* photographic essay, introduction, North Pole Archives.

Here Cupid shows me the sure sign of reindeer love: tails entertwined. The lucky doe is Gisela.

Hhrin, better known as Comet, doesn't like professors. He gave me the high-tail sign and high-tailed it out of there.

Cupid

Cupid gets a lot of ribbing from the other reindeer—but he's big enough that they don't push the teasing too far. Cupid loves to fall in love. In the few months that I was visiting the North Pole, Cupid spent (and made) time with the following hapless female reindeer: Olga, Princess, Priscilla, Juki, Anji, and a herd of others.

Don't get the idea that Cupid is insincere. It's just that when he starts to court a new doe his heart starts to pound in his throat, his hooves start to quiver, and he just loses his head.

When Cupid was a little calf, his mother nicknamed him Johnny-Be-Good, hoping it would rub off on him, but the ploy never worked. Now his dates say that to him. Constantly. It still doesn't work.

But he's sure great on the Christmas sleigh!

Hhrin

Hhrin, or Comet, is presently the fastest of all the reindeer. On one momentous day back in 1932 he took the crown away from his mother, Rita, and hasn't relinquished it since.

Comet is so fast that he's reportedly outdistanced a 747 at full speed—though I must admit that the report is only hearsay. I didn't see the feat, and I'm not sure I would have believed it if I had.

It's also been reported that Comet can carry a heavier load than a 747 can—and that is even harder to believe. But all the reindeer said it was true—there must be *something* to the story.

Comet doesn't like humans other than Santa (and Santa is half-elf). He's even jumpy around Mrs. Santa. As you can see from my picture, I didn't get much of a chance to talk to Comet personally.

Source:
—St. Sternius, *In Cupido Cupido*, Vatican Library, fourth floor, stack 18.

Source:
—Immanuel Velikovsky, *Comets of the Twentieth Century*, New York: Singleweek Publishers, 1938, chap. 12.

When Santa gave Vixen a mirror, she almost loved someone else for a moment—until she got distracted by the gift.

If evolution is right, Feed-bag's offspring will be born with feed-bags over their noses. If he takes the time to make any.

Vixen

One day many years ago Vixen saw herself in a pool of water, and it's been true love ever since. The image in the water was so striking, so beautiful, that it was hard to get her away from it even to eat.

Santa has since solved the problem by buying her a mirror. Here's how the conversation with Vixen went, using an elf as interpreter:

"It's nice to meet you, Vixen."

"I know."

"You're certainly beautiful. Look at that fur coloring!"

"Yes, it's incredibly sleek, isn't it."

"I don't want to get too personal, but do you have a mate?"

"I'd love to have one, but I've never found a prospect that isn't ugly."

And thus it went, for over an hour. She stared in the mirror all the while, watching the interpreter elf out of the corner of her eye.

Don't get the wrong idea about Vixen. She's a wonderful deer, and she's one of Santa's most reliable on Christmas Eve. And the rest of the year she never causes any trouble. She's too much in love to bother.

Source:
—Vixen Fan Club, official history, Juan Pidero (Brasilia, Brazil), president.

Chauncey

Chauncey is nicknamed "Feed-bag," because that's where his nose lives. In one. When Clement Moore was writing "The Night Before Christmas," he was unable to discover through research the name of this deer—so he arbitrarily named him Prancer, because it rhymed with Dancer in his poem. Chauncey isn't very prancy; if he pranced, his nose would leave its feedbag home, and he'd suffer immediate hunger pangs.

The other reindeer have a joke about Feed-bag—all in fun, of course. They say he was born with a feed-bag on his nose. That he sleeps with one on. Even mates with it on. They say that the only time Feed-bag takes his nose out of his feed-bag is when the elves come by to refill it.

They aren't really exaggerating, either. Chauncey even wears his feed-bag when he's pulling the sleigh on Christmas Eve.

Using the help of an elf interpreter, my interview with Feed-bag Chauncey went thus:

"I understand the others call you 'Feed-bag. . . .' " His answer: "Mmummpnch."

"Are you proud to be one of the reindeer that makes millions of children happy every year?" Answer: "Mmmmummppnhmh!"

Source:
—"Surprising Eating and Feeding Records," staff report, Pillsbury Co. files.

Chich, one of the younger elves, likes to spend his free time jousting with brooms.

Rhirh, Chich's best buddy, is also great pals with Blitzen.

Donner and Blitzen constantly have butting contests while the elves are jousting. Donner usually wins—after all, he's higher up in the antler order.

Donner

Donner is German for thunder, and when I visited Donner it quickly became apparent where he got his name. He spent the whole time playing a crashing, head-smashing game with Blitzen, and the thunderous sound of it filled the whole valley.

In fact, before I visited Donner, I mistakenly thought that the North Pole had more than its share of thunderstorms.

Donner is a stout young deer, a constant companion of Blitzen. I never saw them apart in the whole time I was there. And having an interview with them was quite frustrating, because one would often answer for the other.

Donner is one of the few deer who have true vocal cords, and he can utter a sound that will send shivers down your back. He usually doesn't use it unless he's mad, but I was able to convince him to show me. It sounded like this:

"Eeeeeeeeeeeeeeeeeeeeeeeeeeeeeeee!"

It was so loud and shrill that it literally knocked me back on my rear, bruising my tailbone and nearly rupturing my eardrums. It was truly incredible!

Source:
—Dr. Georges Koftski and Mildred Jones, *Donner and Blitzen*, Warsaw: International Polish Press, 1882, pp. xix-xxx.

Blitzen

Blitzen means lightning in German, and Blitzen goes with Donner like peanut butter with jelly. Blitzen is just a touch down the antler order from Donner—but only because he's giving Donner a break. At least that's what he told me.

My inteview with Blitzen was one of the most enlightening of all. He was quite loquacious, in a reindeer sort of way, and he was willing to answer every question I put to him through the elf interpreter. I was surprised to learn from him, for instance, that Rita kept the others in line by switching them with her tail. It was such an insult to be switched by the grand old lady that the deer did just about everything they could to be good.

Blitzen told me he and Donner were twins. They were born simultaneously, nearly finishing off their poor mother.

He also told me that Santa was a little too lenient with the elves, letting them eat too much of the reindeer's food.

"The *elves* eat your food?" I was credulous.

"The elves eat anything," Blitzen answered. "Unless it moves. You've probably noticed that all of us deer keep moving!"

Source:
—Personal interviews, video tape 92, sides 1 and 2, entitled, "Interviews with Blitzen, the deer, interpreted by Rhon, the elf, 1977," in Author's possession.

Creatures of the North Pole

At first glance, the North Pole is a frozen wasteland, notable only for its cold and icy snow. But in actuality the Pole area is teeming with life. In fact, it has nearly as many different kinds of animals as the equatorial jungles of Brazil.

Most of the species of North Pole animals went unnoticed until zoologist Henry S. Hampton began his studies in 1882. Though Dr. Hampton's early expedition to the North Pole went largely unsung, one of my careful research assistants discovered it. These illustrations are taken from his descriptions, as well as my own observations.

Arctic Tern—Small bird that lives in the Arctic nine months of the year. Terns travel in pairs, because one good tern always deserves another.

Snowy Owl—A swift flyer, lives off snow mice and lemmings. Can spot its prey from 5,000 feet up. Flies into northern Canada and Siberia during the winter. Once baby owls are hatched, the shells from their eggs are used as an ingredient in Mrs. Santa's cleansing compound.

The bowtie feathering is found only on North Pole penguins.

Penguin—A native of Antarctica, some penguins migrated to the North Pole during the great southern thaw of 1557. Northern penguins have developed a more distinctive feathering than their southern cousins: just under the neck is a dark coloring that resembles a bowtie.

Snow Mouse—Smaller than North American house mouse, the snow mouse lives to be four to five years old. Skin is covered with tough, coarse hair. Commonly inhabits abandoned lemming burrows.

Snow Mole—An all-white creature that dwells in snowbanks. A numerous species. Survive on the minerals found in snowflakes, though they sometimes eat mice for bulk.

The snow mole's tail enables it to burrow backwards as well as frontwards.

The white rabbit's ears are able to pick up sounds from over two miles away.

Arctic Fox—A small, white relative of the English hunting fox. The arctic fox is wily and fast; it has been known to climb trees and poles when frightened. Travels behind the polar bear and eats its leftovers. In times of great difficulty, lives off bear droppings.

Polar Bear—One of the fiercest mammals of the northern hemisphere. Can grow to 1,000 pounds. Thrives in cold climates. An enemy of seals and fish. Has been spotted swimming up to 25 miles from land. Used to attack Santa's reindeer—until the elves constructed their "Bear Breaker" which snaps a bear's claws when he steps on it. Now bears rarely prowl around the Pole area itself.

White Rabbit—Immortalized in *Alice in Wonderland,* the white rabbit can move extremely fast. Its coloring enables it to disappear into the scenery before one's very eyes. When nervous, the white rabbit thumps its hind feet into the snow. A great many white rabbits live at the North Pole, and the numbers are increasing all the time.

121

Iceworm—A five-inch-long worm with indigo snout, bilbous blue belly, and bulbous eyes, as Robert Service, the iceworm expert, describes it. The head of the iceworm is truly hideous—and the person who looks too long into its eyes will be mesmerized. Even though the iceworm is very small, its bite is extremely poisonous and is often fatal.

Ptarmigans are great eating, whether roasted, boiled, or stewed—but no one better touch Santa's pet ptarmigan!

The idea of earmuffs came from the iceworm, which wears them in its natural state.

Musk oxen are named after the pungent, musky odor they give off when excited.

Ptarmigan—A grouse-like bird that changes from brown to white in the winter. Lives off berries and seeds. Traditionally makes a strange crying noise on the first day of winter.

Musk Ox—A small, cow-like creature with long, shaggy brown hair and hollow horns. Travels in herds of up to 50, composed of one bull and his harem, with their children. Easily tamed, some musk oxen are used as beasts of burden by the elves.

All male walruses, without exception, respond to the name *Wally.*

Walrus—The giant of the North Pole. Male walruses can grow up to 3,000 pounds. Born with a moustache, which is used as mud-strainer. Can swim over 50 miles at a stretch. Live to be 35 years old.

Northern Seal—A large brownish creature, sleek and slick. Some experts have speculated that the northern seal is at least as intelligent as the Armenian Gentra. Santa has taught seals to clap in time to music and count with their back flippers. Loves to swim; also loves to sun itself on icebergs.

Lemming—A small and furry rodent, much like a guinea pig. Tail and ears are extremely short and sometimes almost nonexistent. Lives in snow tunnels in winter. Sometimes migrates *en masse,* traveling in a straight direction over mountains, snow fields, lakes, and streams. Occasionally migrates right into the sea.

Narwhal—An ancient cross between the unicorn and the dolphin, the narwhal has incredible survivability. A mammal that lives in the sea, yet breathes air. The narwhal can grow to 20 feet long, which includes its 9-foot tusk. Males enjoy having fencing contests with their tusks; Mrs. Santa uses ground-up tusks as antidotes for polar dragon poison.

The polar dragon is judged to have descended from the famous Pedra den of dragons deep in the jungles of Brazil.

During the long and lonely winter, the polar dragon periodically emits a sorrowful call for companionship—but nothing ever answers.

Polar Dragon—One of a kind, the polar dragon is one of the oldest living dragons in the world. His fiery breath has long since burned out; at present all he breathes out is smoke and stench.

Talking
to a
Reindeer

Reindeer are very intelligent creatures, but their tongues and mouths aren't formed to enable them to speak either human or elvish. Because of this, they also have difficulty understanding any more than the most basic spoken commands, such as "Here, boy," and "Up we go!"

In order to communicate with the reindeer, the elves have developed, over the centuries, a highly sophisticated system of sign language. By using their hands and contortions of their bodies, the elves can tell the deer just about anything they want to, from "Time for supper," to "Have you heard the latest Ice Nymph joke?"

Shown below are some of the most common signs the elves use, along with their interpretations:

(hands on hips, bent)
"Stop! Hold everything!" (If the elf also takes off his hat when giving this sign, the interpretation changes: "The buck stops here. The does go to the right!")

Reindeer have difficulty with human or elvish speech, but their understanding of sign language is excellent.

(on all fours)
"Get on your mark . . ."

(both arms extended)
"Let me tell you about the one that got away!"

(pointing left hand)
"Get into that stable until you can behave! Now!"

(pointing right hand)
"Hold it down, you rowdies!

(on knees, left hand raised)
1 "Good-bye! Fly fast and high!"
2 (When little finger is down, the sign means: "Roll over!"
3 When index finger is wiggling, the sign means: "Play dead!")

(arms up, hands drooping)
"Ready? Take off!" (Elves are sometimes known to actually leave the ground while executing this sign.)

Sources:
—*Strange and Unusual Signals of the World*, Washington, D.C.:U.S. Signal Corps, U.S. Government Printing Office, 1829, pp. 312-21.
—*Rbrttnsb' Huf*, c. 1644, abridged copy in author's possession.

125

A Very Small Friend

Look very closely at the circle to the left. If you have a good eye, and can stare without blinking, you'll see a moving green spot. That spot is Santa's very small friend, who lives in his beard. The friend is called a Gnuf in everyday language, although in scientific jargon he's known as the *Rameus rampton*.

Santa and the Gnuf enjoy a symbiotic relationship. Symbiotic is a fancy way of saying, "I'll scratch your back if you scratch mine." The Gnuf keeps Santa's beard clean and untangled. That's his part of the bargain. In return, Santa drips crumbs of food down onto his beard to keep the Gnuf well fed. And, of course, the thickness of the beard keeps the Gnuf warm.

Before Santa had the Gnuf, he had to brush his own beard every day. It was a real pain in the kazoo. The beard was so thick and curly that Santa had to have a special brush made, with bristles of stiffened grizzly bear hair. Every morning Santa brushed his beard for ten minutes. It was ten minutes he could ill afford to spend during the Christmas rush. More than once he considered cutting the whole thing off—but the cold at the North Pole made him think twice.

Where Santa Got the Gnuf. Santa picked up the Gnuf when he made his Christmas rounds in 1716. He doesn't really know how it happened. The day before Christmas Santa brushed his beard and all was normal. The day after Christmas when Santa brushed his beard the Gnuf popped out onto the dressing table.

He was smaller than a dot. Santa probably wouldn't have even known he was there, if the Gnuf hadn't shrilled out a scream of pain.

Santa put on his glasses and carefully looked across the table, until he saw the dot that was making the awful sound. It was some kind of small creature, maybe a bug, maybe something else.

Happy Dancer

Gnufs have a peculiar mating ritual, and Santa's Gnuf goes through it like clockwork every 5.2 years, even though no females are near. The Happy Dance starts with a slight shuffling of the feet, followed by rapid waving of the arms, followed by a more frenetic pedal motion. Throughout the dance the Gnuf snuffles with his peculiar Gnuf sound, in a rhythm similar to that in the popular song, "Chattanooga Choo-Choo":

"Gnufa gnuf gnuf, gnufgnufgnuf gnufa gnufa gnuf-gnuf?" and so on.

The Gnuf got his common name from Santa, who named him after the "Gnuf" noise he makes while he sleeps—similar to a cat's purring.

Santa loves all small things—even bugs and children—and he never willingly squashes a bug. He got a small piece of paper and slid it under the Gnuf, brought it up close to his eyes for a better look. It was something not quite like anything he'd seen before. He brought out a magnifying glass. Suddenly it all came into focus.

There on his paper was a little creature with four legs. Each leg had three toes on its foot. The creature was green and scaly all over. Its skin looked kind of rubbery. Its ears were too big for its head. Its eyes were red. Sticking out of its long snout was a long, slender tongue.

127

"I can't kill it," Santa said. "And I can't put it out, or it will die. But how do I feed it to keep it alive? There's no telling where it came from or what kinds of things it eats."

Finally he put it high on a shelf, still on the piece of paper; and beside it on the paper he put a crumb of bread and a droplet of water.

"I don't know what else to do, little friend," Santa said. And he went about his work.

The next morning Santa began to brush his beard. Out popped the dot, squealing. "Another one?" Santa went to get the paper to pick up this new creature. The old one was gone. "No, not another one—the same one, back in my beard." He put it back on the shelf.

On the third morning Santa brushed it out again. "Maybe it likes it in my beard," he said. "And I can't even feel it in there, so it's not hurting anything." He put the paper back up by his beard, and up the Gnuf jumped. It's been in his beard ever since.

The Gnuf is a very quiet animal (unless it's knocked to the floor or table, which never happens now). It's very clean and never causes trouble. And Santa soon learned that he never had to brush his beard with the Gnuf living there.

A Dinosaur. In 1873 a British scientist by the name of Sir Churchton Winchell (the inventor of the donut) learned of the existence of the Gnuf. He made a special trip to the North Pole to find out more about this strange creature. He spent many weeks with Santa, interviewing him and doing gentle examinations on the Gnuf.

His final conclusions were astounding to everyone, including himself. The next year, 1874, he published his study in the prestigious scientific journal *The Anthropological, Anthropomorphical, and Archaeological Journal of Modern and Ancient History*. Following is an excerpt of his findings:

"Through careful morphological studies, including analyses of skin layers, bone structure, tongue formation, brain size, and molecular configuration in the blood, the tentative hypothesis is that *Rameus rampton* can be nothing other than a dinosaur."

Winchell was very careful in stating his conclusions in the journal. But in his personal diary he recorded the following:

"Good heavens! The little bugger is a *dinosaur!*"

Winchell's study was met with a mixture of ridicule and awe. Some members of the scientific community put him off as a crackpot, citing his previous statement that apes had descended from man. But in the matter of the Gnuf, Winchell has been vindicated. Subsequent studies have shown that the Gnuf is indeed the last living survivor of the dinosaur race.

And there is some evidence that he isn't simply a *descendant* of that race! He was almost certainly a personal contemporary of T. rex, brontosaurus, and the mighty cockroach. That would make Santa's Gnuf several million years old, at the youngest!

Sources:
—Sir Churchton Winchell, *The Anthropological, Anthropomorphical, and Archaeological Journal of Modern and Ancient History*, 1874, vol. 66, no. 20, pp. 1123-4.
—Personal observations of the Gnuf, notes in Author's possession.

Where Santa Goes for Summer Vacation

A lot of theories have been put forth as to where Santa goes for summer vacation. For instance, one popular weekly newspaper in the United States claimed a scoop when they said they saw Santa summering in the Bahamas. A prominent Christmas expert has published "secret information" suggesting that Santa likes to go to the south of France for the summer. And one study has even put him somewhere in Nepal during the month of June.

Frankly, all these theories are pure fabrications, created to make the originator a few bucks. (It's a shame that some people feel they must make some easy money by relying on the name and reputation of Santa, but I guess that's just how the world is.)

If Santa doesn't go to the Bahamas or to France or to Nepal, where in the world does he go? After all, he works so hard that no one, anywhere, deserves a rest more than he does!

The truth is that for many centuries Santa spent his summer vacation right at home. He'd put his feet up on his stool and relax, smoking his pipe and reading a good book. The elves took care of all the chores for him and he didn't really have any worries at all.

But then the time came that he felt he needed to get away from it all; he needed a change of scenery. One Christmas, after Santa had made his rounds, he decided to take a little world tour to see if he could find a secluded spot where he could go for his summer vacation.

It didn't take him long to find exactly what he wanted. Right in the heart of Antarctica was a huge volcano, and, surrounding the volcano, with the wonderful warmth it generated, was a lush green valley.

"This is the place," Santa murmured to himself, and he clucked at the reindeer to set down in it. He was delighted at what he found. The valley held no ferocious beasts; it had plenty of wild tropical fruits, just waiting to be plucked; and the climate was ideal.

Beginning the next summer, Santa began to build a personal paradise at the South Pole. His first project was to erect a pole, matching the one at the North Pole. (That's where the name of the two poles came from. One's south of the rest of the world, and the other is north.)

Loading the sleigh with the vacation conveniences is a special challenge. To make sure they do it correctly in good time, the elves go through several rehearsals, pantomiming the entire process. Then, when vacation time arrives, they're able to load supplies for the whole summer in less than ten minutes!

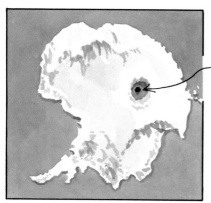

A rough map of Antarctica, Santa's summering place. The volcano is easy to spot from the air.

After the pole was up, Santa built a special little house for himself, some luxurious stables for his deer, cottages for the elves who would travel with him (they go on a rotating basis, so everyone gets a turn), and a South Pole swimming pool, heated by underground hot springs.

The South Pole is dark during the summer months, but the volcano lights up Santa's resort valley.

One Last Thing

As I did my research on this book, I was able to spend over a year with Santa at the North Pole. A month here, two weeks there—it didn't take long for all my visits to add up.

But then it was time for me to say good-bye. Santa is very congenial, but he's a busy man. As much as he loves people, he can't devote much time to visitors.

I felt stronger and happier than I'd ever felt before in my life. It was very sad to think of leaving. But even the best things must end.

I visited with each of the elves for a final time, thanking them for their hospitality. I petted each of the reindeer. When I said farewell to Mrs. Santa, she gave me a loving embrace. I could have sworn a tear glistened in her eye. And then it was time to go.

Santa walked with me as I started out. He put his arm around my shoulders and smiled up at me. "It's been nice having you here, Alden," he said. "You've been a wonderful guest. I've never heard anyone tell a story like you can—not even old Zeeker, and he's in a class all his own."

Then he paused and got a faraway look in his eye. "You know I wouldn't meddle with your book," he said. "You'll know what's best to put in it. But there's one last thing I want to say to the people of the world. If you would, put it at the very back of your book, so people will remember it most."

"I'd be happy to do whatever you ask," I said.

"I know that, Alden, I know that," Santa said. "You're one of the fine people of the earth." He didn't see my

131

blush at his compliment; he was looking out at the snowy horizon.

"Here's what I want to say. At Christmastime, people suddenly turn loving and unselfish. They start to share with others, and they notice how happy it makes them. They give and give and don't really expect anything in return.

"Even nations get the Christmas spirit. More than once I've taken off on Christmas Eve a little worried about the guns and missiles I was sure to encounter—only to find that the warring countries had declared a Christmas truce."

He paused again, and we stopped walking. Santa grasped my arm and spoke more earnestly. "Tell the people that Christmas is the best time of the year—oh, they know that. But why can't we make the whole year like that? Why can't we be loving and sharing all year 'round—even when others aren't loving and sharing back?

"Alden, you know me. I'm not a preachy guy. I've said my piece. But tell the people that, please. Please?" He stared at me for a moment, his eyes not wavering, and then he gave me a great big bear hug. "And tell all my kids that they're the greatest thing on earth," he whispered in my ear.

I hugged him back, as tight as I could. I figured I'd never see him again. But he'd changed my life.

I trudged on through the snow, topped a rise—and then looked back. There was a short, stubby man with a white beard and a wide smile, waving at me. I waved back, thoughtfully.

For months I yearned to see Santa again, mooning for him like a long lost love. Then, on Christmas Eve, I was awakened by someone shaking me in my bed. "Ho! Ho! Ho!" a voice said out of the darkness. I felt the giggles rising up in my throat.

But that's another story. . . .